TOOLBOX PARENTING

TOOLBOX PARENTING

The Most
Practical Guide to
Raising Teenage Boys
You'll Ever Read

GALE A. DREAS, LCSW

SEABOARD PRESS

AN IMPRINT OF J. A. ROCK & CO., PUBLISHERS

Toolbox Parenting: The Most Practical Guide to
Raising Teenage Boys You'll Ever Read by Gale A. Dreas, LCSW

is an imprint of JAMES A. ROCK & CO., PUBLISHERS

Toolbox Parenting: The Most Practical Guide to
Raising Teenage Boys You'll Ever Read copyright ©2006 by Gale A. Dreas

Special contents of this edition copyright ©2006
by Seaboard Press

Address comments and inquiries to:
SEABOARD PRESS
9710 Traville Gateway Drive, #305
Rockville, MD 20850

E-mail:
jrock@rockpublishing.com   lrock@rockpublishing.com
Internet URL: www.rockpublishing.com

Trade Paperback ISBN: 1-59663-518-5
978-1-59663-518-0

Library of Congress Control Number: 2006927037

Printed in the United States of America

First Edition: September 2006

This book is dedicated to
Michael and Andrew.

Thank you for the privilege and honor
of being your mother, for giving me
so much material to work with,
and for allowing your lives to
be out in the public way.
Love you!

ACKNOWLEDGMENTS

As with all worthwhile projects, this one would not have occurred without the support of my "network."

To Mimi Carney and Polly Kosyla, for the backyard barbeque party conversation that began this journey and for your central part in framing out the style of the book.

To Mary Ann Daly, my heartfelt gratitude for your steadfast belief in me and emphasizing the importance of this project, for your wonderful ideas, editing and, mostly your magnificent spirit. Roneen Blank, my thanks for your willingness and eagerness to listen and provide valuable feedback to my stories while sharing our Thai food dinners! To Mary Longe, for your interest in this project, your creative ideas in so many areas, and your wisdom regarding how to market to the target audience.

To Linda Polach, for your valuable long distance friendship, your writing advice and your feedback regarding the worthiness of the material. To Martha Ruschman, for supporting the "normalness" of my stories, for being one of my staunchest cheerleaders, and for catching my spelling error on the title page! To Rich Lessor, my gratitude for your tremendous guidance, wisdom and insight over these past twenty-plus years. To my mother, Helen, for teaching me about the importance of always showing up for your children.

Finally, to my husband Tom Brennan, for your tremendous love, tenacity and willingness to do whatever detail and grunt work was required, which ultimately allowed this book to happen. Your steadfast love, support and sense of humor kept my "pedal to the medal" and your great parenting allowed this to remain a book about "normal" teenage boys with "normal" problems. You are a fabulous father, a fabulous friend, and a great deal of fun to be spending my life with!

TABLE OF CONTENTS

PREFACE

Toolbox Parenting: What Is It?

Think of yourself as a first time contractor whose job is to build a house. Remember, first time, no experience, but the expectation is that at the end of the job, you will have built a house that you can actually live in. Parenting is like that and parenting a teenager is even more like that. What kind of tools do you need to do the job and what kind of tools do you come to the job with?

If you are like most parents, we come to the parenting job with a certain assortment of tools — mostly those we saw used in our own family of origin. In other words, we tend to parent the way we were parented. In most cases, what we learned about parenting did not provide us with enough "tools" to do a really good parenting job, although admittedly, some of us certainly have more and better tools than others. More often than not, however, the "toolbox" we show up with for the parenting job is scanty at best. Maybe a hammer, some nails and a screwdriver. A good start, but not nearly enough to do a good job and sometimes only barely enough to do an adequate job!

By the time our kids are teenagers we definitely need a lot of tools in the box to cover the often particularly treacherous territory involving separation. Because separating from us as parents and learning how to be more independent is the main developmental task during adolescence, it becomes the great parental challenge to figure out how much space to allow our teens to have without losing them. While we certainly know that our children begin to detach from us during the teenage years, we don't want them to detach so much that we are alienated from each other — that definitely breeds "trouble." So, how do we avoid the pitfalls — how do we prepare ourselves for this new developmental stage? We prepare by making sure we have more than enough tools in our box to do the job.

Exactly what "tools" are we talking about? Because the people I work with are often emotionally underdeveloped themselves, one of the first tasks they have to learn is how to parent themselves better so that they can learn to parent their children better. For example, I remember working with one man who was very upset because his son didn't want to play football — he preferred soccer. The dad kept insisting his son play football — because he was big, strong, etc. even though the son kept saying he hated football. Eventually, we were able to get underneath the dad's frustration and understand that it went back to his own high school days when he was unable to play football in his senior year because of an injury. He never got over that disappointment and wanted his son to play football to make up for that. Being able to understand how the dad's own disappointment got in the way of his being able to see what was best for his son, was helpful in resolving this issue in favor of the son being able to play soccer. If the dad had not been able to "get" how he was trying to live out his football career through his son, the ending would have been very different — and not a good one for the son. That's an example of getting a new parenting "tool" — understanding how to separate your "stuff" from your children's.

By the time our children are teenagers, we, as parents, need more complicated tools because the job becomes more complicated. We need to both "upgrade" the quality as well as find new and better tools for the teen years. And sometimes we will simply want to "borrow" a tool from a friend. In this context, these stories are a form of borrowing — we get help from someone who already has the tool and is delighted to let you use it. That's what this is — using some tools that have already been tried and tested. Tools that you can use and put into your own box to pull out when you need them — or tools that you can have "just in case."

These stories are here to provide you with some teaching — some specialty tools needed to do that "slippery slope" parenting through the teenage years.

INTRODUCTION

Storytelling as a Teaching Tool

Why write and why write stories about teenagers? Isn't that a phase we just want to "slog" through and hope that our children — and we — come out alive and basically intact? Why would we ever want to chronicle or reflect on that journey? And how can the mere act of telling stories help in any way? In and of itself, it doesn't. However, storytelling, when done with the intention of using it as a teaching "tool," is a very effective method of learning. How much more interesting is it to learn by doing or being shown than by being lectured to? Storytelling is like that. And how relieving is it when you have been told a story about other people's children that you can relate to your own children? It's like being given a shortcut to an otherwise long and confusing ride. It can help remove some of the worry and fear. Doesn't it help to know you are not "the only one" dealing with an issue? I know how much it has helped me in my life and I'm hoping to be able to offer some of that to you.

My intention is to use storytelling as a way of teaching. I will be using stories about my children, combined with my experience as a clinical social worker to teach parenting skills to parents who are dealing with teenagers. I will be providing a foundation for helping you think through your own parenting style and your own values as a parent by using these stories as a springboard from which to help you clarify or learn new skills which can help you parent your own teenagers. It can also be advice with which you totally disagree. That's okay, too. But at least you will have some concrete opinions and some specific tools that you can take and reflect on — because to be a good parent, you really must think about what kind of parent you want to be and be intentional about it — be "full of thought" about it; be deliberate about it. It's too important a job to do from the seat of your pants, and, most importantly, since our children are our finest treasures, don't they deserve our very best? Use this book to sharpen and improve your parenting skills so that you can deliver your very best to your teenager.

CHAPTER
1

First
Things First

1. One Teen at a Time

When I think about the myriad of parenting styles and approaches, the phrase "One teen at a time" keeps running through my mind. It reminds me of a story about an adult and child walking along the ocean shore. They come upon a scene where there are literally hundreds and hundreds of starfish, stranded on the sand, stuck there as the tide flows back out — stuck on the sand, dying.

Observing this scene, the child runs to the starfish and begins, one by one, throwing them back into the sea. In watching the child, the adult says, "Why are you doing that? There are too many starfish to save. It is an impossible job. Don't bother, it doesn't matter."

"It does to the one I throw back," she replies.

That phrase, "It does to the one I throw back," reminds me somehow of the teen years. It's often a time when kids feel stranded, stranded between dependence and independence, stranded between attachment and detachment. A time of still needing help but not necessarily wanting or knowing how to ask for it. It is a time when guidance is still necessary, but not always desired. It's a time when parenting changes. It's a time, I think, when differences between each teen invite us, as parents, to parent each of them differently, to "tweak" our styles to fit them, and not the other way around. To figure out how to listen to them as individuals and use the "parenting tool box" that we spoke about in an earlier section in a way that honors both the fact that the job of a teenager is to be their "own person" as well as to be "like" their peers. Pretty tricky business both for them and for us!

This prompted me to think about my role as "mom" and, in particular, "mom" to teenagers and even more precisely, a "mom" to teenage boys.

I realized that, as a mom, part of how I have always learned is by listening to others. If I hear how someone else handles a situation it really helps me to use their experience as a springboard for my own. I may decide, for example, that someone else's experience teaches me what I don't want to do, but at least it provides me with a starting place, or a marker, in order to figure out where I want to be.

I remember, for example, when my oldest son was graduating from high school and wanted a graduation party. He wanted his friends to be able to drink at that party. I was appalled at that suggestion until I spoke with other parents who did allow it at their parties. Their thinking was that the kids would drink anyway, so, it was better that they drink where parents could monitor the environment and then make them stay overnight in order to keep them safe.

Hearing their reasoning certainly helped me. I could understand the "trade-off" they had chosen. We still decided we would not allow any drinking at our party even if it meant that none of Michael's friends would show up, but we were very aware that having heard how other parents handled this dilemma helped us decide where to stand for our party. Their "story" helped us create ours, even though the decision we made was very different from theirs. It was just helpful to know what other parents thought about an issue that is ripe with choices and points of view.

Having had that experience, I was struck once again by how important storytelling is with regard to parenting. How much we learn from each other's wisdom as well as each other's mistakes. I thought, then, how helpful it might be to share stories about parenting through the teen years, talking about topics that are often rife with conflict and confusion. I thought that if I learned so well from other people's stories, perhaps other parents could learn from mine. And I also thought about the importance of values and how values shape decisions. When you are clear about what you believe, then the behavior or decisions you make should line up behind these values. For instance, using the example of "to allow or not to allow" drinking at the graduation party, if you believe that your teenager should not drink before age 21 simply because it's against the law, then you line up behind that philosophy when situations come up to challenge your value. In other words, your behavior should match your belief. If an exception to that rule or value comes, up, then you label it an exception and give your reasons for why this is an exception. Otherwise, change the rule to match the behavior. The goal should be to have your behavior reflect what you believe. If it doesn't, you either change the behavior or change what you believe so that you are consistent. Then not only are you role modeling for your teenager, but you're not making decisions based on how you feel or on not hurting your teenager's feelings. You're making your decisions based on your beliefs.

At the same time I suggest that consistency in parenting is important, I also urge having margins — especially with teenagers. How inconsistent is that? The irony here is that they are also learning how to be more adult, so they should be included in on the decision-making that you do. Recently when my 15 year old wanted to go out and hadn't yet done his homework, instead of simply telling him that he couldn't go out because he hadn't done his homework, I suggested he think through the rest of his day and figure out how he was going to accomplish both having fun and getting his homework done. He actually came up with a workable "middle" solution and I didn't have to be "the heavy" and say "no" to him. He figured out for himself how to gauge his time so my job then became one of watching whether or not he followed through. If he did, great, then he's learning about how to manage his time, how to think through getting his stuff done and he's learning about problem solving. And I, as parent, am learning how to step back a little and let him step up.

If he doesn't follow through, then he learns his word can't be counted on and you can then step in and be more controlling because of the lack of follow through on his part. In other words, he hangs himself with his own behavior or he rises to the occasion. As a parent, you have more leverage to move either in the direction of "freedom" or more in the direction of "control." Their behavior helps determine which direction you take. The important lesson here, though, is that you line up with your value, let your teen know what that value is, and include them in on the process. Therein lies both the challenge and the goal!

2. The Book on the Counter

I knew I had hold of something special when I heard hysterical laughing coming from the kitchen. My 15 year old had brought 5 or 6 friends over and they were reading something out loud that had them in stitches. First of all, the fact that they were reading anything had my attention. Then, I was curious not only as to what it was, but also what was so funny. I could always use a laugh myself. So, I went into the kitchen to see what was so funny. I was not prepared for what I saw. I saw 6 teenage boys huddled around the table and one of them was reading a story about Andrew from my manuscript! Imagine my surprise!

I had left the binder on the kitchen counter — the title page fully visible. They had come in, seen it and asked Andrew about it. He told them his mom was writing a book and it was filled with stories about himself and his brother. They wanted to know if they were in any of the stories and when Andrew said "yes," they immediately opened it up — to look for stories featuring themselves, of course! And they went right for the chapters on Drinking, Parties, and Sex. They must have spent a full hour reading out loud, asking questions, laughing and trying to figure out which stories they were in. They were really engaged in the reading and kept saying things like "Andrew, did you really do that? Did this really happen to your brother? Is your Mom really going to publish this? Cool."

I was so surprised by their reaction; it was then that I began to realize how important it had been to chronicle these events. These kids were loving searching for and reading about themselves, and they were fascinated with how and what parents thought about them and these situations. Andrew said a number of times "Mom, that's not how I remembered that" or "I don't remember doing that or saying that" or "I think you got that wrong" or "Is that what you were thinking?" to which I replied, "This is all about my perspective, Andrew. If you want to offer yours, you'll have to write your own book!"

All of which reinforced for me the notion that storytelling was so important. Important for both the storyteller and the listener or the reader. Important for our children to know our thinking, our perspectives, our struggles and our triumphs in raising them. Important for them to see all that goes into the parenting experience; how much love, care, fun, concern, and angst goes into it. And that's just in relationship to "normal" events and normal teenage situations. In written storytelling, not only do our children get to read about themselves and what teenager doesn't want to do that? But, they get to see and understand a little more about us. What we think, how we think, how we care, and how we arrive at the places that we do as parents. And maybe what they get is a little more knowledge and a little more appreciation for us and the job of parenting that we did. And maybe, just maybe, it serves as another bridge to each other — another place of connection — another place where, on some level, our children understand that we do try our best, amidst our mistakes and shortcomings, to love them.

3. Parental Baggage

As I sit here watching the movie *The Divine Secrets of the Ya-Ya Sisterhood,* I am struck by this.

Everyone has it. Some of us have more than others. But we all have to deal with it on some level, especially once we have children. The "it" I'm referring to is baggage — family of origin baggage. We all bring it with us as we journey forward — even as we move on in our lives, further and further away from where we grew up — further away from those who raised us. We move on even as we travel backwards, visiting at different times and bringing forward the influence of where we came from. We bring various pieces of baggage along — the good, the bad and the ugly. The more we understand about those pieces, the more we can choose which parts to hold onto and which ones to let go of, even when letting go is very difficult.

One of my favorite memories from childhood was a simple ritual we had around Christmas. At that time we always got a short, fat scotch pine tree that we would set up in the bay window and let it "open up" for a night before we started decorating it. While it was "opening up," my brother, sister, and I would spend what felt like hours hiding the animals from the Nativity set inside the tree and then taking turns seeing how fast and how many of the animals each of us could find. We would laugh and play or sing Christmas carols all evening. It is one of my fondest memories and is a ritual that I do with my own husband and children. While we don't do this every year, especially since we have an artificial tree, we do it often enough to keep the fondness and warmth of that memory alive. That's good baggage.

On the opposite end is the negative baggage — the memories of too many nights with a father who came home too late, too drunk or who didn't come home at all because he had been in an accident and was in the hospital. These kinds of memories and experiences have their carryover too. They show up when I can't reach my 18-year-old on his cell phone, or he doesn't have his cell phone and he hasn't arrived home when he said he would. Or when my 15-year-old goes out with friends and neglects to tell me where he's going or when he'll be home and now it's dark out and I haven't a clue where he is. Normal kinds of things with normal children in normal families that mostly have normal endings — endings where everyone is fine and nothing terrible has happened — no one is drunk or has been in an accident; they just forgot or lost track of the time — normal. But for me, because I wasn't raised in "normal" around these things, I go to fear — heart-pounding fear, agitated worry, imagining the worst. I visit any and all of these to a greater or lesser extent — because that's what I was used to — that's what was normal for me. Not only was that normal for me with regard to my father, but it then became the norm with my brother and then with my sister — the triple whammy. Normal was extreme — drunken or high episodes; fights; arrests; visits by police; stumbling to bed or not making it home at all and watching my worried and frantic mother looking out the window or calling friends or going outside to "look" for my brother, sister or father.

Although only an observer of that activity, the price I paid was one of defining normal as something to be frightened of and something that carried danger with it. So, in my adulthood and with my own children, I have to redefine normal and not treat them to my fear, but treat my kids with my trust, which they deserve and which they have earned. I have to filter through my past and remind myself that the life I'm in now is not the one I was raised in. I have intentionally created a different life — a happier one — but sometimes that gets cloudy. When it resembles the past in any way, it gets very cloudy and at those times I have to remember to stay in my current life.

I have shared these experiences with my kids because it helps them to understand me when I overreact or get "paranoid," as they call it. I have in part, been defined by those past family experiences, but I have also used them to carve out and repair some of that damage, not simply to repeat it. I'm sorry that it's even something that has to come up at all — but it does. And I do know that when this "bad stuff" does come up, I can remind myself that these memories are part of a suitcase that I need to empty out and replace the "old stuff" with positive experiences or "good stuff" from my current family. My one consolation — and it is a big one — is that when the bad memories surface, I know that they are only a place I will visit — they are no longer a place that I live.

TOOLS USED

1. Acknowledge that where you came from has both a positive and negative impact on how you parent your children.

2. Try to separate out which elements belong in the past and which belong in the present.

3. If one of your teens behaves like one of the black sheep in your family of origin, don't assume your teen will end up that way and don't treat him as if he already has.

4. Don't let fear be your guide, especially if your family of origin life was unhappy.

5. Do be mindful of carrying good things from your past forward into your current family.

6. Make sure your "baggage" holds only what you want and need in it, not old "stuff" you no longer need.

4. Family Mission Statement

Our family has a Mission Statement. By that I mean a set of beliefs/values that we, as parents, operate on, as a way of helping us navigate through and identify choices and make decisions that might otherwise be very difficult to make. And we pass this Mission Statement on to our children.

I can remember, for example, when my kids were very young and my husband got a call from a friend and neighbor, asking him if he would be interested in another job. This job would have been very interesting, a step up in career, twice the pay, and would have required out-of-town travel at least one-third of the year. Well, Tom and I sat down to talk about it and the talk lasted about five minutes. Would the extra money be great? Yes, it would. Would he enjoy the work? Yes, he would. Would it be exciting and a good career move? Yes, it would. Would he take it? No, he wouldn't. Why not? The only drawback would be the third of the year out of town. What would be so bad about that? Nothing — *except* for the fact that the travel collided with our family value of being home with our children during their growing years. And because we had been very definite about that value after having children, making the decision to say "No" to this job was very clear. Not easy, mind you, but very clear. If we had said "Yes" to the new job, then we would have had to change our family value to line up with that "Yes" decision. We would have had to say that being home with the kids was not as important as making more money or making a new career move. The clearer and more articulate you are about your beliefs and values, the more quickly and easily these decisions become when they arise.

Like Tom's decision to decline that new job, I remember making a career decision based on family values as well. Being a Social Worker, I had been accustomed to working three or four nights a week running groups, teaching classes and doing individual therapy. And I loved doing all of it. When I became a parent, however, I knew I had a decision to make. If our family value was to be home with our kids, then working four nights a week was in direct conflict with that value. Like Tom's decision, it was not easy, but it was very clear. To be in sync with that value, I said "No' to a lot of opportunities that came my way because of our Mission Statement.

A family Mission Statement should have two important features. 1) It should be articulated, that is, you should be able to say aloud what it includes. Consequently, it would probably also be beneficial to write it down so you can see it and be reminded of it. 2) Be deliberate about your Mission Statement. If you say something is important to you, then your behavior should reflect that importance. For example, if talking respectfully to one another is part of your Mission Statement and you are always yelling at each other, you are out of integrity with your statement. Either change the value or change the behavior.

The beauty of a Mission Statement is that is really does help you clarify and identify your priorities. If you "line up" behind those priorities, great. If you don't, then it is probably time to re-examine your beliefs and values. Either way, knowing what the belief is, in the form of a Mission Statement, helps define the behavior.

If you haven't created a Mission Statement by the time your kids are adolescents, don't panic. The nice thing about this is that you can create and implement one at any time. Chances are you already have one but have never formally stated it aloud — you may be acting on one without knowing it. I'm suggesting you create a formal Mission Statement now, especially if your kids are teenagers, since navigating as a parent through the teen years is so much more of a challenge.

Some of the areas to consider in creating a Mission Statement include, but are certainly not limited to the following:

1. Communication style. Do you want to be a parent who is able to listen to everyone, talk civilly, respect one another's

viewpoint? Or do you want to be authoritarian — a "Don't talk back to me" or "Do as I say, not as I do" kind of parent? You can be either, just claim it and know that whichever style you choose has a set of positive and negative consequences that go with it.

2. Time spent with your kids. Do you want to be a parent who is actively involved with your kids or a step removed? Do you plan on being home regularly with your kids or home intermittently? Obviously, our choice was to be regularly and actively involved. You may make another choice. You just need to know which one you are choosing and be clear about it. Don't say you'll do one thing when you actually do another. Teens *do notice* if you are consistent in what you say and what you do.

3. Family rituals. Do you want to be parents who have a lot of rituals? This might include regular family dinners, weekly/biweekly nights with each child, regular church attendance together, annual holiday rituals, family vacations, and so forth. Or do you prefer to be parents with few rituals? Again, whatever you pick, just be clear and deliberate about it and know that what you reap is what you sow.

4. Spirituality. Do you want to be parents who have a particular religion that you want your kids to practice or do you want them to make their own choice about religion/spirituality? Again, one is not necessarily better than the other, but you need to claim what it is you value and then practice it.

I'm sure there are many other areas that you can include, but these four examples provide an idea of how to create a Mission Statement with values in a way that helps you live a family life with a foundation upon which you may all rely. There is comfort, security, clarity and guidance in this approach. By the time your kids are teenagers, having a Mission Statement can truly help you better navigate through the ambiguity and difficulties presented during adolescence. It also sets an example for your teens to develop their own Mission Statements as they mature and move toward independence.

CHAPTER
2

Talking
To Your Teen

1. Is the Cup Half-Full or Half-Empty?

Last year, I attended my then 16-year-old's varsity basketball game against a local high school. It was a big rivalry and our team was the anticipated underdog. Michael was totally psyched for the game, and I was totally psyched to watch it. He was a starter and was very excited because he knew a number of our friends were going to be in the audience and were there to see him play.

Well, two minutes into the game, one of Michael's opponents stepped on his foot, thereby twisting Michael's ankle and, in a flash, Michael was out of the game. He had twisted his ankle — badly. The team trainer looked at it and soon came up to us in the stands telling us he needed to go to the emergency room. I went down to tell Michael we would have to leave the game in order to take him to the ER. He refused, saying it was important for him to stay at the game so he could support his teammates. The ER could wait. I could see how important it was for him to stay — could see how angry and frustrated he was at not being able to play; and I figured, since the harm was already done, why not let him stay till the end? So, he did. He sat at the end of the bleachers with ice all over his ankle, screaming his support to his team-mates from the sidelines.

Interestingly, the player who had taken Michael's place in the game had been one of the five original starters on the varsity team — until Michael came along this year. So, this player hadn't got-ten the playing time he was used to getting, and I'm sure didn't feel great about that. He did a great job in this game, and our team won the game in double overtime. It was quite exciting.

After the game, I drove Michael to the ER. He was delighted that his team had won the game, but he was also really furious that he had gotten injured and was unable to help the team to victory. I knew we would be unable to have a rational discussion about the game until Michael had released all of his rage.

So, I suggested that, while we were driving to the ER, he just

yell out, swear, scream — do and say whatever he needed to re-
lease his anger. He looked at me like I was nuts and said, "Are you
sure?" I said, "Absolutely. Just imagine this guy is in front of you
— what would you want to say to him?"

Well, it didn't take any more than that to get him started. He
started yelling, swearing, screaming, name-calling — anything
and everything that came to his mind. And I kept encouraging
him to keep yelling — I even joined him at a few points of his dis-
course, yelling and swearing myself. He finally got to a place where
he was laughing — and so was I — at the ridiculousness of it — he
had gone so far over the edge that it was even funny to him. And
what a difference it made!

By the time we got to the ER (Thank goodness it was a long
ride!), he was in pretty good spirits and seemed to be able to reluctantly revel in the victory rather than focusing on his lack of
playing time.

While we were waiting for him to be taken care of, I asked
Michael if he would be willing "to think about what had happened from another perspective."

He sort of cocked one eye up, anticipating that this would be
yet another one of his mother's loony ideas, but said, "O.K., if
you must."

I then suggested that perhaps there was a spiritual perspective
in the midst of this occurrence. That maybe, just maybe, his getting a sprained ankle allowed another player to have his shining
moment. The other player was a senior and would not have many
more games in his career, while Michael was a junior and had yet
another year to play. That perhaps, just perhaps, Michael's sprained
ankle was a gift to this other player. That the other player needed
to play — to show his stuff and build his self-esteem — more
than Michael did. After all, Michael did replace him as a starting
player, which must have been a blow to the other player's ego.

Michael rolled his eyes at this, but reluctantly admitted it made
him feel better to think about it that way.

I have no clue about the reality of that perspective, but I did want Michael to get the point that there's more than one way to think about something that looks and feels only negative. You really can choose the perspective you ultimately live with — and frankly, which one is going to feel better? The positive one, I think.

TOOLS USED

1. When your teen is angry, don't try to talk him out of it.

2. Listen to him — encourage him to let you know what he is angry about and how angry he is.

3. Remember that listening to him doesn't mean you are agreeing with him.

4. When you listen to him, he will be better able to hear you later.

5. After he's finished being angry, ask him if there is any other way to look at the situation.

6. Suggest lessons he might learn by considering your perspective or a different, spiritual perspective.

2. Conversations — or Lack Thereof

It happened sort of slowly, I think, although it felt like it happened overnight. One day it struck me as my 8th grader came thru the door after my saying, "Hi Hon — how was your day?" and getting the response, "Fine" — followed by his retreat to his room.

This is all I get? I think. *Away from me all day and this is all I get?* Then I slowly realized that this kind of response had actually been happening over the last number of months — I just hadn't noticed. Then I wondered, "Where did my real son go? The one who would come in and chat, unsolicited, or would come in and ask how I was doing, how my day had gone? Where did that son go?"

And then I realized he was gone — gone to teendom where privacy, secrecy and monosyllabism reigned supreme. And I felt sad — at first. Then I felt mad and decided that some parts of this I could do something about and would. So, I gathered my teenage sons into the kitchen and started "The Talk." The talk was aimed mostly at Michael, who was 13, but I included 10 year-old Andrew so he could get a heads-up and get an early start on mom's expectations in "teenagedom."

So, "The Talk" began.

"The Talk" consisted of a lecture really, regarding my expectations of the boys when it comes to conversations. I refuse, I said, to accept monosyllabic grunting as an acceptable form of communication. At its very base, it's simply rude behavior. And rude behavior was unacceptable. While I accepted the fact that Michael was now a full-fledged teenager who needed both space and privacy, I did not accept that that meant he would behave like a caveman or a moron.

Nope. Completely unacceptable.

Instead, I expected at least sentence fragments, if not complete sentences when he was asked a question. If I didn't get some semblance of that, I would be following him around, asking and probing until I got an acceptable amount of information.

"You want too much detail," said Michael. "I just want to give you highlights and you want me to fill in all of the blanks."

"That's absolutely right," I say. "I do want details and I deserve to have them. It's polite. And also, let me just tell you that unbeknownst to you, giving me details is actually preparing you well for future relationships with women. Women love details and the sooner you get that, the better off you will be. So, understand that I will expect that from you. I want details and once I get them, I will leave you alone. If I don't get them, I will torture you and ask, ask, ask until I do get them. So, it behooves you to give me the info up front. Then you are free to go back to monosyllabic heaven with your friends and anyone else you choose to behave that way with. But I expect details!"

"And furthermore, when your friends come into our house, I expect them to say "Hello Mrs. Brennan, how are you today?" or something that actually sounds like a greeting and not simply a head nod or grunt or comment like, "Mike home?"

"If I get that then I promise to then leave you alone. If I don't, I promise to pick at you until I get what I want — understood?"

Well, after that day I must say, I did get more of what I wanted. As a matter of fact, the next day when Michael came home from school, I said, "Hi Michael, how was your day?" In response, he sat down and launched into a three-minute synopsis of his day, compete with great detail and lots of information.

At the end of his description, he said, "OK, mom, I did it. Was that enough detail for you?"

With delight, I said, "Absolutely. Yes — I loved it. Thank you for paying attention and giving me what I asked for. Now I'll leave you alone and won't have to come trailing after you, begging for tidbits of information."

He got what he wanted — to be left alone — and I got what I wanted — a connection with him.

Now I can't sit here and tell you that that happens every day. It doesn't. But it does happen enough times that I'm basically satisfied with the level of information I receive. When I don't feel like it's enough, I dig around for more. Sometimes I get it and sometimes I don't. But clearly the boys understand that, like it or not, they live with a mom who requires a certain level of data entry from them and without it, they will be plagued with questions until I get it. And we can also laugh together about how "high maintenance" I am when needing details. My response is "Absolutely! I AM high maintenance — and proud of it!"

TOOLS USED

1. Talk to your teenager every day.

2. Ask questions. i.e. How was his day? Who does he hang out with? What was his most interesting class today? Does he have a lot of homework?

3. Don't let him "slip away" without talking to you. Let him know you are interested in what he has to say.

4. Talk about current events at your dinner table and ask for his opinion. Don't accept "I don't know" as a response.

5. Tell him what you want/expect from him regarding communication.

6. Use humor/kidding as a way to get him to talk.

7. Tell him about your life, too, and let him know how you spend your time and what is important to you.

3. Halloween and Teenagers

I love Halloween with little kids and I hate it with teenagers. For the past three or four years, we have had some sort of drama happen on Halloween. I would just as soon skip this holiday until my children are old enough not to be interested in it.

This year my 17-year-old, as well as my 14-year-old, got into "it" with other groups of kids from the area. We happen to live in a multi-cultural, multi-racial neighborhood, which brings with it, of course, a certain degree of tension and a certain degree of jeopardy regarding safety. This year both groups were "strutting their stuff" and ended up throwing words, eggs and shaving cream at each other. Later, after everyone's feathers had been sufficiently ruffled, one group ended up hitting my 17-year-old and his friend on their way home. And, of course, my Michael, with his sense of self-righteousness, thought he had absolutely no responsibility for any of these activities.

And, of course, in theory he is right. In practice, however, he did contribute to what happened to him. However, I almost made the mistake of saying that to him at the wrong time. The wrong time, in this instance, was right after it happened.

He came home hurt and upset. He was furious that this had happened to him and was filled with righteous indignation. From my point of view, he had gone out looking, on some level, for trouble. And he had found it. Now he was mad — probably because he was the one who got hit instead of the other way around.

I had to work really hard to zipper my lip. I wanted him to understand that variations of this same incident had happened on the previous three or four Halloweens. Michael might rationalize the first mishap but not repeatedly, year after year. I was sure that, in some way, he was contributing to these confrontations.

But, I sat on my tongue and — believe me — it was hard work. I managed to tell him how very sorry I was that this had happened to him — which was true. I was glad he wasn't really hurt.

I waited until the next day. I asked him to just think about what he might have done differently to avoid this confrontation. Naturally, he kept sticking to his point about being right — and having the right to be wherever he wanted to be. I agreed with him but added, "You can be right, Michael, but sometimes being right can get you hurt or even killed. And sometimes being right can make you act stupid. I think putting yourself outside on Halloween after this has happened to you three times is stupid, stupid, stupid."

While I think he did hear me, I'm sure he did not agree with me at all. We settled for a stalemate along with my suggestion that he think about being in a protected place the next time Halloween comes around. I don't know that he will heed that advice, but I certainly cross my fingers that he will.

TOOLS USED

1. Don't let your teenager out on Halloween unless he is going to someone's home.

2. Drive him wherever he needs to go.

3. Have a party yourself and let him be under your watchful eye.

4. Check on him regularly to make sure he is not pursuing trouble and trouble is not following him.

5. If something negative happens, don't forget to listen to his perspective. If you don't listen to him, he won't listen to you.

6. Review the decision-making process your teen went through and the consequences of his choices. Discuss both the positive and negative consequences.

CHAPTER
3

Integrity
Issues

1. Honesty

It was Saturday night and Michael was out with friends. His "usual" routine was to check in by phone sometime during the late evening and either come home around 11:30 p.m. or stay overnight at a friend's house. This particular evening, he didn't check in and wasn't answering his phone. At this point, the "parent antenna" begins to go up. By 10:00 p.m., still no word, so calls begin to friends' parents. No one has heard from their child and attempts to reach other kids by phone fail. Red flags are now up. Finally, around 10:30 p.m., I hear from Michael. He says he didn't think he had to check in because he spoke to me at 6:00 p.m., right before we were meeting friends for dinner. That wasn't my assumption.

He then "announces" he will be staying overnight at his friend's house. I say "No" — he is to come home. He protests and says, "No — he's staying overnight." And "Why do we have to be so paranoid and call everybody's parents?" he demands. I tell him he's to come home and he hangs up. I talk to his father and I have Tom call him. He tells Tom he's not coming home. We call him back again and tell him he either comes home or we will come and get him. He's being disrespectful and belligerent and will come home.

At this point, Michael says he can't come home. We ask him why. He says "I've been drinking. I can't drive the car."

We tell him his dad will go and pick him up. Tom does just that. Michael gets home, comes to see me and says, "Congratulations. You caught me. But you have to give me credit for not driving. I did act responsibly."

I agree, saying that part of his decision-making was a good choice and that we'd talk more about it tomorrow. For now, he was to go to bed.

The next day we sat down and talked about it. Michael's position was that he drinks periodically, that he only has "a few," that he never drinks and drives and he never rides in a car when someone is drinking. From his point of view, he is behaving responsibly. Furthermore, in comparison to his other friends, his drinking is "no big deal."

"You have no idea what I say 'no' to — you should be grateful that I only do the little that I do."

"I'm grateful," I say, "but drinking is still illegal. We don't want you doing it and you will have consequences as a result." He was grounded for two weekends for this behavior. He was also very annoyed at us because he thought his honesty should override any consequences. We told him it only saved him from worse consequences.

TOOLS USED

1. Insist on honesty and you are more likely to get it. Also, make sure you give honesty in return — you can't expect to get it if you don't practice it yourself.

2. Even if your teen is honest with you, there should be consequences for negative behavior. The fact that he has been honest does not cancel the consequences for misbehavior. These are two separate issues. Thank him for his honesty but don't absolve him from paying the price for a poor choice.

3. Give your teen credit for whatever level of honesty he provides you. Let him know it does help in extending trust in the future and perhaps in mitigating the degree of consequences.

2. Cheating

We were stunned when the Spanish teacher phoned. Andrew had been caught "almost cheating ... getting ready to cheat" right before a test. If he hadn't been caught prior to the test, he would have cheated. But he was caught with his "cheat sheet," handwritten in pencil, on his desk. There was no formal procedure, since the test hadn't started, and therefore no negative consequences from the school.

"Too bad," I thought. Maybe he should have been totally caught. Frankly, I was ambivalent about it. Part of me was relieved because Andrew's reputation would stay intact. Part of me was sorry that he didn't suffer more negative repercussions from the school as a reminder of his failure of integrity.

While he didn't suffer any negative consequences at school — and did, by the way, pass the test without cheating — he did have some disapproving feedback from us. First it was the family talk, filled with questions like "what were you thinking?" and "where was your integrity?" and "how did that feel to behave like that?"

His answers included "I wasn't thinking ... I didn't have enough time to study because I watched the Cubs in the playoffs instead," and "It was stupid of me and it was no big deal." After being sufficiently clear that Andrew understood the violation of trust as well as the breach of his own integrity, we talked about consequences.

He was to be grounded on the weekend and also had to write a note of apology to his teacher for putting her in the position of "cheating police." He did show sufficient remorse and seemed to understand the moral issues and character breaches. We were satisfied that he understood what he had done, how disappointed in him we were and what we expected of him in the future. As parents we learned, once again, that our children are not above breaching their values and he learned that those breaches are much bigger than they appear to be at first glance. The appeal of trying to pass a test the "easy" way has many more repercussions and guilt feelings than he ever imagined — if he had thought it through in the first place, which he didn't.

We also learned that we needed to be more vigilant in supervising his homework. It appeared that he was willing to skimp on his study habits in the short run. Ultimately, this resulted in his making a poor, fear-based choice when confronting the reality of his unprepared state.

We wanted him to see the wider picture of being prepared for life with his integrity intact instead of looking for shortcuts that tempt him to compromise on his values. At this point, around this issue, lesson learned, and consequences paid.

TOOLS USED

1. Call cheating what it is — a breach of integrity.

2. Talk about integrity in terms of impact on reputation over the "long" haul.

3. Explain the difference between doing things the "easy" way vs. doing them the "right" way; i.e. if you begin to compromise or rationalize choices in small ways, it gets easier to do about the big issues.

4. Make sure you talk about your own integrity and any struggles you have had regarding choices you have made.

5. Don't let him get away with the attitude "It's no big deal — it was only a test," or "Everyone does it." Everyone doesn't do it and it is a big deal!

6. Give him consequences for the behavior regardless of whether or not he was "caught."

3. Bullying and its Consequences

He thought it was funny — no big deal. I was appalled — appalled not only that my son would do such a thing, but, even more, appalled that he didn't think what he had done was wrong.

What was the "it?"

"Pantsing."

My son "pantsed" another student in the school lobby prior to the beginning of gym class. Yep — pulled the kid's pants and boxers down "as a joke" in front of a bunch of other students. And thought it was funny. Didn't mean to pull the boxers down, too, but still, pretty funny, he thought.

It wasn't funny, however, to the student he did it to, nor was it funny to the teacher who observed it. Andrew was reported and subsequently brought before the Dean of Students for disciplinary action. The punishment was a one day in-school suspension, which Andrew felt was unfair. Unfair because "lots of kids do it and nothing ever happens to them. It's what guys do." He was having difficulty taking any responsibility and was getting caught on the fact that other kids do it and nothing happens to them. At least, that is the case in the world according to Andrew! He also indicated that other kids had pulled this same stunt on him (and vice versa) and it was "no big deal."

What he was missing, however, was the fact that this time the student he did it to did feel bad ... that it was, in fact, a big deal to this person. The student felt humiliated and embarrassed and was having a hard time letting it go because other kids were now making fun of him as a result of this incident.

So, as parents, where did we stand on this? First we got information. Information from Andrew and information from the Dean. After listening to all of it, we concluded that this really was an act of bullying and Andrew needed to learn that his behavior was very inappropriate and that the punishment did, in fact, fit the crime.

When Andrew came home from school, we sat him down to talk. We asked him how he felt about what happened and what he learned from it. He said he still felt that the punishment was unfair — that other kids had done pantsing and never had any punishment. But he also understood that what he did resulted in hurting another student. Even though he still didn't think it was a "terrible" thing to do ("It's not like I brought a gun to school"), he did "get" how his behavior humiliated someone else.

He also felt, however, that having apologized several times to the student was punishment enough. The school disagreed, saying this kind of behavior would not be tolerated and an in-school suspension was an appropriate punishment.

We agreed, although it was very difficult. Andrew obviously felt badly and strongly disagreed with the punishment being "inflicted" on him. But we felt that this was really an example of a larger issue — that of breaching personal integrity. Andrew had been caught "almost" cheating a few weeks before this and we looked at both incidents as prime examples of Andrew behaving outside of his personal integrity. We talked to him about deciding what kind of person he wanted to be — one who could "get away with stuff" in order to get a better grade or get a laugh or get peer approval. Or did he want to be someone who could be proud of who he was, whether or not anyone was looking? We suggested that his moral compass was "off" and he needed to get it back on course.

We asked him if he was behaving in a way that felt good to him and if he wanted to be known in this way. He said "no," that this behavior was not who he wanted to be and that he learned his lesson. This experience did not feel good and he would definitely not be doing this in the future.

After listening to him, we, too, felt he had learned an important lesson about himself. But we also felt he needed some more time to think about what he had done and what he needed to do to change. We informed him he would be grounded for one weekend. In addition he had to write three letters of apology — one to the student, one to the teacher who observed the behavior and one to the Dean. He accepted it all quite willingly, saying, "I expected that to happen."

That told us we were on track with our thinking.

It saddens me to see my son have to learn some of these lessons the hard way, but I'm also aware that learning them the hard way is still about learning them. It is a great deal better than not learning them at all.

TOOLS USED

1. Teenagers make mistakes that are sometimes embarrassing to us as parents. Separate your embarrassment from their actions. They did it, not you.

2. Listen to their perspective. Let them tell you how they viewed what they did and why.

3. Give them your perspective on their behavior.

4. Ask them if they understand why they are being punished.

5. Ask them what lessons they have learned from this experience.

6. Suggest lessons you think they should learn or you want them to learn from this experience if they don't get them on their own. Decide on a reasonable punishment you may need to add to any outside punishment.

CHAPTER
4

How
They Look

1. Body Image

Looking good is definitely an important value in our house. I know that by virtue of the amount of time spent both in the shower and in front of the mirror. Facial products have taken on new prominence and expense — not only acne cream, but the cleanser and the toner and the "spot" reducers, to say nothing of the shaving "gel" as opposed to the shaving cream. And let's make sure we have the right deodorant and "anti-stink" soap as well as a wide variety of cologne products. And don't just squirt one little squirt — no — make sure you squirt your shirt, and your face and then give a couple of squirts in the air that you then walk into — you can't smell good enough! Never mind that anyone within six feet of you is left gagging on your splendid cologne choice!

And let's not forget about hair gel. First one has to find the absolute right product — actually, anything that's cheap doesn't seem to work as well as any expensive brand. Gelling doesn't seem to take up that much time, once you have the right product, but the most time consuming of the primping process is definitely the shower. I am amazed and baffled at how long a boy can spend in the shower — they have no notion of what a five-minute shower is. And when asked what could possibly take so long in washing only one body, they both say you have to make sure to get all the parts and not just once because they sweat a lot.

On the other hand, I am totally puzzled at their reluctance, resistance and repulsion to taking a shower at school. They would rather smell to high heaven and have their "balls stick to the side of their legs" (their words, not mine) than be naked in front of other boys. No, they wouldn't consider taking a shower in their boxers — too nerdy — and no, having a towel around them up to the second they go into the shower would never work, either, because they are simply not going to be nude in front of other boys — that's it — the end — doesn't matter how nice the facilities are; it simply isn't going to happen. I continue to just shake my head at this and wonder if this too, is just a phase, or a permanent paranoia. I suppose looking at their dad, I can foresee them outgrowing this as well — and feel hopeful — especially since I am often riding in the car with them after their basketball games and the collective smell of the group is not one you want to be around for long, particularly when they try to disguise it by throwing on cologne — definitely gag material!

TOOLS USED

1. Notice hygiene — or lack thereof.

2. Don't necessarily comment — unless with humor.

3. Ask if you can purchase any special products, when you are "going to the store anyway."

4. If their hygiene is so bad that it's difficult to be around them, let them know that.

5. They may ignore you, but invite them to notice how other kids, (and adults!) may be avoiding them or standing far away from them because of their body odor.

6. Tell them how great they look and how much you appreciate seeing them take good care of their appearance.

7. Even if you don't agree with how they look, compliment them on taking care of their appearance.

2. Body Piercings

When I least expected it, my 17-year-old came home sporting an earring. He had just returned from a week in Kentucky where he had volunteered, through his Jesuit high school, to help build a house in one of the poorest sections of the state. He had gone with 19 other students, mostly girls, to do this service work.

Proud as a peacock I was, to think that my son was giving a week of his "highly-earned free time" in summer to give back to those in need. My biggest concern in his absence was imagining him with 15 girls and five boys and not once did it cross my mind that I would be purchasing earrings for him upon his return or that he'd be going through mine.

When asked why he didn't feel the need to check this decision out with his parents, he said he didn't think he had to. "After all," he said, "I am 17 now. I will be going off to college next year, making my own decisions. Why not start practicing now?" Bad timing is what I thought. Let's wait until you actually go to college, shall we? I'm not sure I'm ready for his decision-making to begin, sans parental input.

At any rate, I was just still getting used to his new look when he abruptly removed the earring. He apparently took quite a lot of razzing from his friends to the point where he decided to take the earring out. I didn't have to say a word and, I must admit, I'm a bit sad not to be able to share my earrings with him or take him shopping for his own.

TOOLS USED

1. Don't sweat the small stuff. Even if you disagree with what he decides, don't get bent out of shape about it. Chalk it up to the learning curve.

2. Don't assume you know your son and that he won't surprise you with the things he says and does — in either a positive or negative direction. Expect to be surprised.

3. Be ready to listen to why he made a particular decision.

4. Go through the pros and cons of your teen's decision, emphasizing the positive and negative aspects of how he arrived at that decision.

5. Remember, this kind of situation becomes an opportunity to teach your teen about how to make decisions and living with the ones you've made.

CHAPTER
5

Around
The House

1. TV Time

This is definitely a struggle in our household and that struggle is not one the kids have, it's we parents. I admit to not liking TV too much, although I must also admit that I am an intermittent watcher of the daytime soap opera General Hospital, which I have watched on and off for over 20 years. Having said that, I wish our children would watch less of it than they do. But, here's the dilemma. My children both hate to read. Oh, they'll do it for homework and they are both good students, but they will rarely, if ever, read for pleasure. Tom and I are sometimes convinced that they were switched at birth since he and I both love to read and never feel like we have enough time to do it. Also, we read to them constantly as children, so their reading repulsion is a mystery to us. I think maybe it's testosterone-based. Tom thinks it's a possibility, since he swears he never read much until he was out of college. I suppose I should be heartened by that. I still find that hard to believe, since he is such an avid reader, but then I didn't know him in those days. Hence, my even stronger belief that it must have to do with hormones.

It might also be related to the fact that reading is a quiet activity and requires movement of the eyes as well as actual thought work. TV, on the other hand, requires only a prone position, with slight hand movements with the remote, followed by staring at a screen. This they seem to be able to do for significant periods of time. So, what do we do?

Well, as parents, we do intervene during the school year, saying we refuse to raise male "slugs" who only know how to talk about TV shows or grunt monosyllabic responses to questions. During the school year, we "insist" on no TV from Monday through Thursday, so that schoolwork can be done and done well.

In theory, this works well. In practice, there are always exceptions. Exceptions like, "There's no school tomorrow, so I can watch TV tonight and finish my homework tomorrow during the day."

Reasonable, right? Or should we simply stick to the rule and say "No."? Maybe we should, but we don't. We let them watch, wusses that we are.

Then there's the exception of "I finished all of my homework, so can I watch TV?" Reasonable, right? Or should we stick to our guns? Again, maybe we should, but we don't. Oh, we certainly try. We suggest, "Why don't you read ahead?" Or, "Are you doing your best at school or just good enough?" We toss these lines out, hoping this will get them thinking. And actually, to be fair, our older son, Michael doesn't watch nearly as much TV as our younger son Andrew. Andrew is someone who could probably recite verbatim, every commercial on TV. He may never know who Melville or Einstein are, but he will know more products from commercials than you or I could possibly remember. I'm not sure if I should be proud or appalled.

At any rate, this feels like an ongoing dance that we do — Tom and I encouraging them to read more, them insisting that they already do enough of that in school and that they "deserve" to do what they enjoy — namely watch TV. And I suspect that, as long as they continue to do well in school, we will simply have to agree to disagree.

TOOLS USED

1. Try to have a general rule about T.V. We say T.V. is off Monday through Thursday until homework is finished.

2. If spending too much time "playing," turn it off.

3. If exceptions occur, i.e. off days, field trip days, etc., give some margin. Teens tend to give a little more if they feel they have gotten or "won" something.

4. TV can be watched so long as grades are maintained.

2. Chores

I had absolutely reached my limit. Walking into 13-year-old Andrew's room, I was barely able to see him through the pile of clothes, books, shoes, and God knows what else on the floor. I resolved in that moment that he was going to get better at keeping his room in order if it was the last thing I did.

While discussing with him about his room, it became clear that my value of cleanliness was different from his value of being able to control his own space. Besides, he insisted, he knew where everything was and he liked it messy — it made him feel good.

Well, it makes me nuts, I tell him, and I think we have to find a compromise. It's one thing, I say, if it's just your room that's messy, but it's another when that style begins to spread to the rest of the house, i.e., dishes left wherever they were eaten, towels left on the bathroom floor, Popsicle covers and sticks left on the table, sticky and wet, with no concern at all for who might come after him.

He and I resolved that once a week he would "pick up" his room but that it would not have to be as clean as I would like it, and that, in relation to the rest of the house, the general rule would be to "look behind you" and if you've made a mess, clean it up. How does this work? Pretty well — at least I'm doing less nagging than I used to — and that may be simply because my own standard of "clean" has lowered — all in all, not a bad compromise!

TOOLS USED

1. Let your teen know that he is part of a household and, as such, must participate in the running of that household by performing tasks.

2. Have a margin around how a task is done — better that it is done fairly well without parental criticism than done very well with a lot of parental criticism.

3. Prepare your teen a few days ahead of time if you want him to help you with special household projects.

4. If a teen has a hard time doing chores, do them with him. At least it's time together even if you're doing more of the work than you want to. The goal is certainly one of having teens do chores independently. However, it does no harm if "getting started" requires that you do some of the work alongside your teen. It's certainly better than getting into a heated argument where both of you are angry and nothing gets done anyway.

5. If you expect teens to do specific and regular chores around the house, provide time frames in which to do them. For example: make sure your room is clean by Noon Saturday; the dishes must be put away by bedtime; the garbage must be taken out by 10 p.m.

3. Sleep Time

My kids would sleep until afternoon if I let them. And, to me, the question is, should I let them? On one hand, I think — they work hard as students all week long — have to get up at 6:15 every morning in order to get to school on time — participate in extracurriculars after school — then homework. It's a long week and they don't get nearly the amount of sleep that they need.

On the other hand, I think, "These lazy boys — how dare they think they can sleep all day? There's work to be done." I have to work all week long too and there's plenty to do around the house that they should help with. Besides, being in a household means everyone should be participating in its running. Unfortunately, I don't always feel that way. I often feel like kids should be allowed to be kids, which means they should be able to go to school, come home, do homework, and just hang around, or have friends over and hang out. Sure, they should also help around the house, but not to the point where I become a drill sergeant and they feel like boot camp recruits.

I keep striving for a middle which, to me, looks like the boys being able to look around them and see that something needs to be done and do it — not have to be told to do it. For example, when putting your dirty clothes in the laundry, notice the other dirty clothes there and put in a load of laundry by yourself — don't wait or expect me to do it.

Or notice the dishes in the sink and put them in the dishwasher or empty the dishwasher when the cycle is done. I would love that kind of responsible and anticipatory thinking rather than the Gestapo approach to household maintenance. I keep trying to teach that kind of "how to be a family" behavior, but I'm not sure it has any staying power. I'm heartened whenever I notice it happening and think that, maybe, this might become habit-forming. However, that thought often goes out the window the next time I see the pile of dishes in the sink or the laundry halfway up the laundry chute. In the meantime, I'll keep preaching about it and keep trying to decide whether I wake them up mid-morning on Saturday and Sunday and tell them they have to report for duty — or else.

TOOLS USED

1. Let kids sleep in on weekends — you get more out of them if you do.

2. Make deals with them. For example: "I'll let you sleep until 11 am, but then you have to cut the lawn or clean your room or help your dad or, or, or..."

3. If they don't follow through with the tasks after you have agreed to let them sleep in, then bring on the consequences and make sure you follow through.

4. Make sure you sound matter of fact about the consequences, as if, of course there will be a consequence for failing to perform the agreed-upon task. For example: "I'm sorry you decided not to cut the lawn. I guess you won't be going out tonight. Maybe next time you'll follow through with your agreements. I did my end — I let you sleep in. You didn't do your end, so now you have a consequence. I sure hope you make a different decision next time, so that you don't put me in a position of having to impose a punishment on you."

5. Thank them when they do what is asked of them. Let them know you appreciate it when they cooperate and that healthy families behave in this manner.

4. Money

I don't think we have done a very good job teaching our kids about money. Why do I say that? I say that because both of my children still tend to think that money sits in banks simply waiting for us to enter the drive thru lane, put our deposit slip in for as much money as we want, and drive off, ready to spend, spend, spend. Or write a check when we need something — or pull out the plastic. In their minds we have an endless supply of money at our disposal and they need only ask to receive. They don't seem to have grasped the relationship between earning, saving and spending.

Oh, we've tried at various times to talk about working, saving and spending and to various degrees we have reached some modicum of success. Andrew earns money by mowing lawns and squirrels his money away in various hiding spots in his room, preferring to spend his parents' money rather than his own. And both children reluctantly put half of their earnings and "special occasion money" into the bank. But it doesn't really mean much to them, probably because they can't actually "see" their money. It feels like it's just money that is taken from them.

We've never had an allowance program and stuck to it. With good intentions we would start one, give them $5, $10 or $15 dollars a week and warn them "Remember, when this runs out, there is no more, so make sure you budget what you spend." But inevitably, there would be a special occasion or necessary expense of some kind or we would simply forget to give the allowance and slowly our good intentions gave way to giving money when needed or requested with occasional visits to accountability. I fear our children will lapse into being plastic users with little sense of how money works and will fall into bankruptcy or parent rescue schemes as they go through their adulthood. We still keep trying, however to pepper our handouts with lectures and wisdom-filled information about how to be smart about money.

We did establish a rule that, while our sons were in college, we would agree to pay the college costs, but the boys would be responsible for spending money and books each semester. And, since 19-year-old Michael has been in college, he has been quite good with managing his money. He knows that whatever money he makes during the summer is his spending for the school year, so he's greatly improved at budgeting. Clearly our kids have learned the most about money when they have been responsible for their own spending.

I hear other parents talk about teaching their children about investing and saving and budgeting and I lament that we have been well-intentioned but sporadic in our guidance in this area — our sons still don't understand the ins and outs of money as much as we would like them to. However, we have improved our communication by clarifying our financial expectations and our sons have gotten better at meeting and following through with those expectations.

TOOLS USED

1. Teach children about money early.

2. Give them an allowance and hold tough when they run out and ask you for more.

3. Make a stock investment with your children and use it as an example of teaching them how to make and track an investment.

4. Stick to a "half and half" principle — half of special occasion money gets put into a savings account or invested in some way. Show them statements so they can "see" where their money is and how much they have from month to month.

5. By the time teens get to college, they should be familiar with how to make and stick to a budget.

5. Online Usage

Thirteen-year-old Andrew and his friends had been online in a chat room, talking with various friends and friends of friends. During one of their communications, one of Andrew's friends said, "I'm going to kill you if you say that again." Someone unknown to us who had witnessed this statement reported it to AOL. AOL, in return, cut us off immediately from their service. We called AOL to unravel the sequence of events and eventually our service was restored, but only because of a technicality. We were told if it happened again, our service would be cancelled.

We spoke with Andrew and he, in turn, spoke with his friends about who had done the deed. We, in turn, spoke with the father of the boy Andrew had made the statement to, just to inform him of what had happened. Andrew was lectured about the protocol of AOL and what language was and wasn't acceptable to them and he was told not to be in chat rooms anymore. So, he did stop that behavior. However, he apparently started visiting "other" sites.

During a routine computer "clean-up," our technician informed us that while cleaning up the computer, he noticed that a lot of pornography sites had been accessed over the past number of months. In looking at the dates and times, it was clear it was happening at night and over weekends. And there were a lot of them.

We sat both of the boys down and asked them if they were going to porn sites. Both of them denied it, until we looked at a printout of the "cookies" on the computer and went over dates and times, etc. Michael admitted "sometimes" looking at sites and sometimes doing it when his friends were staying overnight. He also said that once you got into a site, it was really hard to get out of it, hence all the "cookies."

We discussed the whole idea of pornography and the use of women as objects in these sites. We also talked about it in relation to getting addicted to these sites and how inappropriate they were for them at their age. We talked about having relationships with girls and how looking at pornography can certainly color how they look at and treat women as they are growing up.

We informed them that we would be putting a restriction on their Internet use and that they would be unable to access these sites anymore. While they understood our thinking, I'm sure both boys felt that, as usual, their parents were overreacting. Our perspective, however, is that we were just doing our job of monitoring them at a time when they were unable to monitor themselves and/or believed that their behavior didn't really require any monitoring at all.

TOOLS USED

1. Monitor what your teen is doing on the computer.

2. Check the "cookies" on the computer to see which sites your teen frequents.

3. Put parental restrictions on which sites your teen can/ cannot go.

4. If porn sites are an issue, then talk to your teen about what it means to look at women as "objects' and how that can influence his relationship with girls and later, with women.

5. Talk to him about respecting himself and girls enough not to engage in that kind of "diminishment."

6. Talk to him about what being "respectful" sexually means at his age — i.e. getting to know a girl as a friend and not just thinking about her without her clothes on.

7. Discuss what you consider "reasonable" time on the computer.

8. Encourage activities that engage your teen in interactions with others, especially if the computer is being used extensively for entertainment.

6. Curfew

Fourteen-year-old Andrew had gone down to the lakefront with two of his friends. He had called to check in and said he would leave the lakefront at 8:30 p.m. and walk home. I asked him when his friends had to be home and he said 8:30 p.m. So, I told him to leave with his friends so he would be home at 8:30 p.m. as well.

At 8:50 p.m. there was no Andrew and no call. I called his two friends' homes and they weren't home either. Some relief in that, but, being a "nervous Nelly" kind of mom, I was constantly looking outside to see if his familiar form was walking home. Nope — now it's 9:10 p.m. — not late, really, but unlike Andrew not to be on time or in communication. Finally, at 9:15 p.m. he calls to say that George's sister would be picking them up and taking them home. Whew! I'm relieved.

When Andrew comes in we talk about why he wasn't home at 8:30 p.m. like he said he would be. He replied that because I told him not to walk home alone, he was staying with his friends and going home with them. Apparently, the 8:30 p.m. curfew was a flexible time to Andrew since he had focused in on the "walking home with friends" and I had focused on the "8:30 p.m." portion of the conversation. So, we agreed there had been a miscommunication — I was thinking one thing — he another and that, next time, we'd try to be clearer. I think we'll be getting him a cell phone, so I'll feel better!

TOOLS USED

1. Younger teens — earlier curfews. Older teens — later curfews.

2. When kids come in, make sure they come and see you in person, face to face. This gives you a chance to check for any drinking/substance abuse.

3. Be flexible with curfews and special events. If you give a little, he is more apt to cooperate at other times.

4. Check in with your teen during the course of the evening; know where he is and with whom. If your teen changes locations, tell him to inform you of the change.

CHAPTER 6

Siblings

1. Sibling Quibbling

I remember a time when my boys were arguing fiercely with each other in the basement. They were about 13 and 10-years-old respectively, and were very competitive with each other. If one said white, the other said black — if one said it was 10:00, the other would say, no it's 10:01. They simply refused to find any common ground. I had recently read an article in Ann Landers' column that addressed this issue, so I decided to try what she suggested.

I went downstairs with the article in my hand. I told the boys to sit down, that I had something important to say to them. I explained to them that I was disturbed at listening to them constantly argue and disagree with each other and that it made me nervous for their future. I reminded them that they don't have many family connections and that when their father and I are dead, they will basically only have each other and if they continued to treat each other this poorly, they wouldn't have each other either.

I then read the article to them and asked them to think about it. I told them it behooved them to find a way to be friends with each other — to find a way, somehow, to value each other, because they might be the only family they ultimately had. My older son said, "Hmm, good point, Mom — never thought about that — but, you have to admit that Andrew is the most annoying person I know because he's always provoking."

From Andrew's point of view, Michael was always putting him down, so the one way he could get back at him was by provoking — it made him feel good.

I must say, though, having that talk did make a difference — I don't remember seeing or hearing them go to that level of "meanness" anymore. Don't get me wrong here — this doesn't mean they're wonderful to each other all the time. They're not. It does mean, though, that they do tend to be mostly respectful of one another. One of the other turning points in this arena was when Andrew was the lead in his 8th grade play. We made Michael go see his brother and when the intermission came, Michael turned to me and said, "Mom, Andrew is really good in this — I can't believe that's my brother! I could never do that!" What I think he learned was that Andrew actually had some skills that were different from his — Andrew was good at something that Michael wasn't. That event did seem to be a turning point in their relationship because Michael actually had some newfound respect for Andrew.

Three years later, it's really nice to watch them be able to play basketball with one another, to drive in the same car without arguing, to carry on a conversation that isn't antagonistic, but respectful, and for them to actually have a lot of fun together. I do find a lot of comfort in knowing that they have been building a very strong friendship, not a rivalry, and when they do get competitive, it's on the B-ball court and not in all area of their lives.

TOOLS USED

1. If your teens fight a lot, share your concerns about the long-term negative affects.

2. Find the Ann Landers article or some other written information on sibling fighting and read it to them.

3. Compliment them anytime you see them getting along.

4. Encourage experiences that require them to cooperate with one another, i.e. domestic tasks, sports, etc.

2. Older Brother Advice

I wanted a videotape of the moment — older brother giving advice to younger brother. And I wanted it recorded because it represented one of those rare moments as a parent where I felt I actually didn't have to say a thing — that what was being offered was wisdom and I was delighted that I was not the one giving it. Not only was I not the one giving it, but, had I been the one offering the advice, it would have gone in one ear and out the other. As it was, this advice was definitely going in one ear and staying put.

We were at dinner together, talking about the fact that basketball tryouts were coming up in a few weeks. 17-year-old Michael was already assured a spot on the Varsity team. 14-year-old Andrew, however, as a freshman, had to tryout and was uncertain whether he would make it. We started talking about how Andrew should prepare for this experience. Right away, Michael looked at Andrew and started imparting his suggestions.

"Listen, Buddy, if you want to make the team, let me tell you what you have to do. First off, don't fart around. Be serious, don't goof off, listen to the coach when he talks, and above all, don't put that stupid smirk on your face at any time. It looks disrespectful. You can have fun — you're supposed to have fun — but you also better take it seriously or they won't take you. There are too many kids who want to play, who may not have the talent you do, but may make up for that with willingness and determination. If you don't do all of that, you'll end up watching these games from the stands, not from the basketball floor."

I was truly impressed with Michael's impromptu advice and obviously so was Andrew because he was paying strict attention and wasn't arguing with Michael. He did try a couple of times to "Yes, but..." him. However, Michael just held his hand up and said, "Shut up and listen." So Andrew did. And so did Tom and I. It was reinforcing to see them interact like this — older and younger brother — one trying to help and advise the other.

It ended with Michael offering to spend some time with Andrew in the alley, practicing some basketball moves. Whether or not Andrew makes the team, what came before it was heartening and reinforcing. Wisdom can come from many directions and sometimes the wisest thing a parent can do is to be silent.

TOOLS USED

1. Ask the older sibling to advise the younger one if they have experience in the issue being discussed.

2. As a parent, keep quiet by letting them have their own discussions.

3. Thank the older sibling for passing on his/her wisdom.

3. Sensing Trouble

One day we received an e-mail from one of 16-year-old Andrew's coaches. In it, the coach said he had noticed a change in Andrew over the past few weeks and the change was not positive. Andrew was being disrespectful and was hanging around with kids who tended to get in trouble at school. Was it OK, he asked, to talk to Andrew about it?

OK? Not only was it OK, it was wonderful that he had brought it to our attention so that we could be aware of and address it from our end as well. So we told the coach how grateful we were that he had not only noticed this change in Andrew, but had taken the time to notify us as well as being willing to talk to Andrew about this negative change in behavior.

We decided to talk to Andrew that night. We gave him a copy of the coach's e-mail and asked him what his thoughts were about it. He read it and made some non-statement, shrugging his shoulders, saying, "I don't want to talk about it. I know what to do and I'll do it. Just leave me alone. I'll be fine."

We said, "That's not good enough. We want to know what's going on with you that you would be behaving like this in the first place. Let's talk about it."

At this point, Andrew simply blew up. He started yelling, "I don't want to talk about it. You always want to talk about stuff and I don't want to — do you get that? I don't want to talk. I'll do what I need to do. I know what I have to do and I'll do it — just leave me alone!" Then he promptly put his head down on the kitchen table.

After initially being stunned by this outburst, I responded by saying: "It is *NOT* OK for you to just go away from us and *NOT* talk about this. It's not like you to behave like this, so something must be going on and we want to know about it. We are going to stay here with you until you decide to talk about it."

Andrew responded to this admonition by keeping his head

down on the table, saying nothing. I, then, decided to go over and put my hand on his shoulder. At that point, Andrew began to cry. And cry and cry some more. He just sobbed. So, Tom and I went to him and put our arms around him and he cried even harder. He must have cried for a solid 20 minutes, during which we just held him and basically, said nothing. When he was finished crying, we all sat down and we asked him if he was willing to talk about what had just happened. He said "Yes." When we asked him what HE thought was going on, he said, "I really don't know. I only know that I'm really sad, but I don't know why."

So, we started asking some questions. Was it alcohol or drug related? No. Friend related? No. School related? Maybe. Did it have anything to do with following in the shoes of older brother Michael? Yes, he thought that was part of it. Did he think that maybe it had to do with not knowing who HE, Andrew, wanted to be rather than who he felt he was SUPPOSED to be either from his parents or his teachers or his coaches? Yes, he thought that was a part of it too.

After listening to his thoughts and trying to help him clarify and articulate what he was experiencing, we asked him if he thought it would be helpful if he went to talk to a counselor about what was going on for him. He said "Yes, he thought it would be a good idea." We then asked him how he felt about sharing all of this with us and he said, "Surprisingly, I feel better." We just pointed out how talking about things and feelings can be so much more helpful than acting them out or coming out sideways with them. He agreed. We talked a little more, agreed on a plan of action, hugged and ended our discussion.

Andrew started weekly therapy sessions the week after this discussion and within a month of these sessions, was feeling much better. Four months later, he is still in therapy and not only likes it, but is finding it very helpful in both understanding himself better and behaving in ways that have more integrity for him.

TOOLS USED

1. Ask your teen about any behavior changes, whether you notice them or someone else does.

2. If he is reluctant to talk about what's going on with him, be persistent. Don't let him get away with monosyllabic responses or ignoring you. Keep pressing.

3. Use touch as a way of reaching him.

4. If he is unsure of what is going on, suggest some reasons YOU think he has changed. Often, he really doesn't have a clue and it's up to us to make some connections for him. Look to recent events in his life, or yours, for information to help you.

5. Get professional help if you think he could use additional assistance. Don't be afraid or ashamed to seek additional guidance for you or your teen. Remember, it takes a whole "tool box" to raise a child! And sometimes that toolbox includes other adults or professionals outside of the family.

CHAPTER
7

Sexuality

1. Where Does Sex Fit In?

I must admit to having not much of a clue about where my 17-year-old son is in relation to expressing his sexuality. Because he has not had, at least to my knowledge, a steady girlfriend, I don't think he is yet sexually active. I do know that he has kissed girls and had some crushes, but I've never heard or seen any evidence of sexual behavior — and believe me, I have been on the lookout. And while I would be surprised if I were to find out he is sexually active, I have learned not to be astonished or to ever think, "My son wouldn't do that." I now know better. I don't think that my teens are going to be the exception to the rule. I'm not always going to know what my child is doing and he's not always going to be doing the right thing.

Regarding sex, we continue to bring up the topic — usually at the dinner table — as a way of either informing our children of what we think or believe in regards to sexual behavior, or trying to find out what they think and feel about this subject.

I recall one dinner conversation where we brought up the topic of oral sex. I had seen Dr. Phil on Oprah. He had a number of teenagers on and they were describing the prevalence of oral sex — particularly girls giving oral sex to boys, in grammar school as well as high school. I was flabbergasted, realizing that I was totally unaware of any such "trend." I promptly taped the show so we could talk about it later. That night at dinner, I told the boys I had watched this show and how amazed I was at it. I asked them if they knew anything about this oral sex trend and if they had engaged in it themselves. My 17-year-old nearly dropped his fork, saying, "I can't believe you want to talk about oral sex with your children at the dinner table!"

Undaunted, I told them Dr. Phil encouraged all parents to be asking and talking to their children and that I was simply taking his good advice. Well, after their initial incredulity (and after my husband allowed that he would have preferred that I had shared my dinner topic "plans" with him prior to the event), we ended up having a very interesting discussion. Both boys were aware of this happening, although Andrew, who was in 8th grade, said he didn't think it happened at his school. Seventeen-year-old Michael was very aware of it. He said he didn't know if it went on in the school, but was aware that most kids doing it didn't really consider it to be sex — they thought kissing was more sexual than oral sex. Shocked again, my husband and I seized this opportunity to educate the boys about the sacredness of sex and how indiscriminate sexual behavior diminished the specialness of it and also jeopardized their physical safety.

The next day Michael went into one of his classes, "Peer Helping," and told his teacher what he talked about at his dinner table the night before. To his credit, the teacher suggested he bring the tape to school. Michael did that and the class spent two sessions discussing oral sex. I never did get the details about exactly what they discussed, but I was delighted that it was being examined in school as well as at home.

We haven't yet run into any particular experiences regarding sex, so our approach continues to be one of sharing our own views of sexual expression, which is, mainly, save it for partners you love, use protection at all times, and treat your partner with the utmost respect. We also present articles from the paper, or other TV shows — anything that keeps them mindful about how to choose wisely when it comes to sex. I'm sure there's much more in store for us on this topic; but, for now, preparation seems to be the order of the day.

TOOLS USED

1. Start talking to your teen about sex before he becomes a teenager.

2. Tell your teen what your beliefs are about sexuality and what you want for him.

3. Ask him about what kinds of sexual behaviors are happening at his school, including oral sex, intercourse, etc. Chances are he won't tell you, but ask anyway.

4. Don't be afraid to talk about sex out loud. He doesn't know as much as he tells you he knows.

5. Bring up sex as a subject with some regularity.

6. Congratulate him on making good choices when he tells you he is not doing anything inappropriate.

7. Watch videos with him, give him written materials, or read materials with him so that you feel better about the information he has been given.

2. More-or-Less-on Sex

After looking at the Table of Contents of this book, I realized that I didn't have enough information about sex. So., while we were on a family vacation, I thought I'd bring up the subject.

We were having lunch in an outdoor café and I announced to the boys that I wanted their help with something. "Sure," they said, "what do you need?"

"What I need," I said, "is another story about sex."

"What!" they said in unison. "Are you serious?"

"Yes, I am perfectly serious," I said. "I don't have enough material in my book on sex so I thought this would be a good time to ask you where you were on this topic and then include it in the book. After all, you're almost 21- and 18-years-old now and it would be helpful if I had more information about what's going on with you. We could talk about it and then I would write about it. I don't want to feel like I'm being deficient either as a parent or to anyone who is reading this book. I want to feel like I have done a thorough job of covering different and difficult subjects and sex is one of those subjects. I'm wondering if your Dad and I should have talked more about it with you."

Well, the boys just looked at each other and then looked at their Dad and they all started laughing. I gave Tom the evil eye, then, for joining them and he said, "Don't look at me! I'm staying completely out of this one. This is between you and them!"

And the boys said, "No way, Mom. We are NOT giving you any more information about sex. You can put this under the topic of "it's no longer any of your business! Suffice it to say that we've heard what you and Dad have preached about for years regarding sex and that's all you need to know. If we need you for anything, WE'LL ask YOU. Do NOT ask us!"

While said in humor, I knew they were not kidding. I did continue to try different ways of asking for details, but continued to run into closed doors from both of them as well as a "It's between you and them" response from Tom.

So, what did I do? After a few more thwarted attempts, I finally — and reluctantly — decided to surrender to their decision. It was clear they were going to give me nothing. However, before I gave up completely, I did manage to reiterate our beliefs about intimacy, appropriate vs. inappropriate sexual behavior along with the overall topics of making sure they were friends with whomever they were sexually active with, never objectify women, practice safe sex, etc. I was doing my best to throw it all out there at once. They "half" listened to me but continued to shake their heads. I was left wondering whether we had covered sufficient sexual information territory to carry them through the often very nebulous and tumultuous waters of sexual intimacy. I guess I'll just be left wondering and hoping that we did the job well enough for them to navigate on their own.

TOOLS USED

1. Continue to ask your teen about his sexual behavior even if he insists on not sharing any details with you.

2. Let him know that he can come to you at any time with questions and/or concerns.

3. Remind him about what your beliefs are regarding intimacy, sexual behavior, establishing relationships with women, etc.

4. Don't be afraid to bring up the topic. If, at some point, he doesn't agree with you, he will at least know what your beliefs are.

CHAPTER
8

Driving

1. Car Accidents and Consequences

I knew it would be just a matter of time before it happened and of course it did — the first car accident of the teenage driver. My 17-year-old had just come back from a week of volunteer work and this was his first day driving in over two weeks — first mistake. I should have warned him to be careful driving since he was a bit rusty.

He had also been out late the night before visiting with friends he hadn't seen in two weeks and had to get up early the next morning, so he was driving tired — second mistake. He was driving our "best" car rather than his own because "his" car was dirty and gasless — third mistake. Can you see where this is heading? While he was not plugged into these "predictors," one of his parents should have been.

Luckily, he rear-ended someone at a traffic light, just when everyone was beginning to accelerate — everyone, except the person in front of him. And, he insisted, he had done everything right. "Everything?" I said.

"Well, almost," he admitted. He actually made it sound like it could have been my fault that he hit someone. "You were the one who taught me to check my blind spot," he says. "I was looking to change lanes and was checking the blind spot, when I ran into her. She stopped suddenly and I was making sure no one was in my blind spot, so I could change lanes."

"So," I said, "it sounds as though because you were checking your blind spot, which I taught you to do, and she stopped suddenly, it shouldn't really be your fault because you were doing all the right things."

"Well, sorta," he said. "I am really sorry. I didn't do it on purpose. I really was trying to be careful, and was just doing what you taught me."

"Well," I said, as I gazed at the car's crunched hood and the shattered headlight, "I'm thinkin' that maybe, just maybe, you weren't doing all the right things. Like, maybe before you accelerate, you just might make sure you're looking in front of you and not behind you. What do you think about that?"

He reluctantly agreed, but still thought his apology and admittance would be enough. "Is that all?" he asked.

"No," we say. "There are still consequences to your behavior. This accident will probably cost us about $1,000 to repair. How did you plan on assisting in that?"

"Well, I don't know how I can. I don't have a job and I start school this week, so I can't help out."

"Exactly," I say, "so perhaps the solution is for you not to drive for a while. For how long, I don't know but at least for a while." This had shaken his confidence so much he seemed actually relieved not to drive and we were content to have him "hoof" it for awhile or have friends pick him up as reminders that driving a car really is both a privilege and, more importantly, a responsibility.

TOOLS USED

1. Make sure you drive enough with your teen to be confident in his driving skills.

2. Talk about what to do in the event of an accident. Discuss calling the police and what to expect. Instruct him to always call home, etc.

3. If an accident occurs, talk about it calmly. Don't get into "whose fault this was," but do talk about accountability and responsibility.

4. Establish consequences for the accident, if necessary, and make sure to follow through.

2. Driving

It was Halloween. Michael was 16. He and a group of friends decided to drive to a local park with shaving cream and eggs in order to have some "harmless" Halloween fun. Another group of kids from another area had the same idea. For a while, each group of kids at the park was keeping to itself. Then (inevitably) someone from one group started throwing eggs at kids from another group and pretty soon they were yelling and threatening each other.

In the midst of this, Michael asked a friend to move his car so it wouldn't get "messed up" with egg and shaving cream. Michael was covered with shaving cream and didn't want to dirty the inside of the car, so he asked his friend to drive. Just as she began to move Michael's car, the "other" group of kids began to threaten Michael's group. They got into their car and managed to cut off Michael's car, causing an accident. Michael began screaming at the other driver, who immediately reciprocated with elevated threats. Each of them was having a "testosterone moment." Suddenly a third car pulled up, the occupants of which were friends of the "other" group. One kid emerged with a baseball bat in hand.

Michael got appropriately scared, forgot about the need to be "macho," promptly jumped in his car and drove off. He waited an hour before calling us and never did call the police.

We had him come home immediately. After hearing Michael's side of the story, we asked him "At what point did you exercise good or bad judgment in this scenario?" He thought he did pretty well across the board, except for getting out of the car and into a verbal sparring match with the other teen. We congratulated him on what he did do well, but suggested he might have done a number of other things, mainly to have stayed away from that park altogether, especially on Halloween. His point was that BECAUSE it was Halloween, going to that park was precisely the thing to do —

besides, he said, it was mostly harmless fun — until the accident, of course, which he saw as not his fault at all. Just unfortunate — and expensive and potentially dangerous, I added.

TOOLS USED

1. Make a rule: Under no circumstances let anyone else drive your teen's car.

2. Tell your teen not to get out of the car to fight with someone else. You never know if a weapon will appear.

3. If there was an accident, instruct your teen to call the police.

4. Set parameters on whether or not your teen can drive other teens around and how many.

5. Go over the "events" of the night in detail, emphasizing areas where your teen exercised good judgment and places where he exercised bad judgment.

6. Use the experience as a "teachable moment," not a "blaming" moment.

CHAPTER
9

Drinking,
Drugs,
and
Smoking

1. The First Drinking Party

It was the end of 7th grade and Michael had asked if he could have a party with about seven friends followed by a sleepover in the yard on the last day of school. We said yes. He spent a number of days preparing for the event: cleaning, mowing the lawn, setting up tarps, putting electric cords up so they could watch TV, etc. We were thrilled; delighted he was taking so much responsibility for this event. Ha! Little did we know what they actually had in mind!

On the Friday night in question, one of the boys' mothers received an anonymous call from what sounded like an adult, saying, "Do you know what your kids are up to tonight?" She pressed for more details as well as the identity of the caller, but to no avail. She called me and reported the information saying, "What do you think we should do?"

I suggested waiting and watching, thinking it would be better to "catch" them at something than to either head them off at the pass or accuse them of plans about which we had no real evidence. So, early in the evening, Michael received a phone call from a girl and I decided to put my detective skills to work and listened in on the conversation. It was pretty typical — questions by the girl met by grunting responses by Michael. That is, until the conclusion of the conversation. The girl asked "Are you going to do anything tonight?" Michael answered, "I don't know yet — it depends on my parents and how much they're going to be checking on us."

O.K. So, here was the inkling of evidence that foul play was potentially on the horizon.

After the call, I reported the information to Tom and we devised a strategy. The kids had some fireworks, so Tom would take them down the alley to supervise the lighting while I agreed to go in the yard and rummage through all the backpacks, looking for evidence. Feeling like I was doing something sneaky, but willing to do it anyway in service of the "greater teenage good," I went crawling around the backyard tree house, looking for booty! After about five minutes of rummaging through clothes and school supplies and gum and videos, the clink of bottles in one of the packs drew my complete attention. Opening the backpack, I saw two bottles of wine, a couple of beer bottles, a few cans of beer, tobacco and cigarettes — certainly enough alcohol to get these kids "buzzed."

What to do now?

I decided to take the backpack in the house, went and got Tom on some pretext and informed him of the "find." We decided we would contact every parent and have them come over, then bring out the evidence with everyone present.

So, about 15 minutes later, cars started pulling up in front of the house and you could hear the boys saying, "Hey Mike, what's going on? Why are our parents here?" And one of the boys could be heard saying "Hey, where's my backpack?"

With seven kids and seven sets of parents squashed into the basement, the "fully stocked backpack" was brought into the center of the room, and the question was asked, "Does anyone know anything about this?" while one by one, the wine, beer, tobacco and cigarettes were pulled from the backpack. A stunned silence from the boys — they all looked like deer in the headlights! After a bit of a wait, one of the boys confessed, "That's my backpack. I did it."

When pressed further he said "I had someone outside of JJ Peppers go in and buy it for me."

As we were listening to this story, I took another good look at the alcohol and thought that this story wasn't lining up. The confessor was obviously trying to take the fall for the group. All of the alcohol was "odd and end" — no six-pack — two cans of this and two cans of that. Looking closer at it and at the wine, a slow light began to go on in my head. That alcohol was looking too familiar. I said, "Wait a minute" — and went to look in the garage refrigerator. Sure enough, that alcohol looked familiar because it had come from our own refrigerator!

Coming back to the group, I confronted my son, "OK, Michael, what's the real story here?" And slowly the details came out — sneaking a few cans or bottles out during the course of the week. Their plan was "just" to get a little buzzed in the yard to celebrate the end of the year.

What was really powerful at this point was the wonderful job all the parents did, as a group, to talk to the kids about a violation of trust, about lying, about using parents' good will and abusing that privilege. Each parent then took their teen, had them apologize to us, and everyone went home. Each parent set up their own set of consequences for their sons.

We then had a lengthy conversation with Michael about addiction, how pervasive it was in each of our own families of origin and how "at risk" Michael is, just in terms of the gene pool. We also informed him that he would no longer have the freedom during the summer that he thought he was going to have. He had to go to summer school from 8:00 a.m. until noon every day and had to take the "L" to and from. So much for having a lazy, carefree summer! While we were both very disappointed about this event, we were also very proud of the way that we and every other parent handled it. We used it as a teaching moment and we were glad that no one got hysterical. The boys really got a lesson in suffering the consequences of their choices and we got a lesson about not being immune from our children making stupid decisions. As we perform our parental duties of trying to steer teens down the "right" path, this situation reminded us that mistakes are part of the picture — it's how we handle them that can make all the difference.

TOOLS USED

1. Don't believe everything your teen tells you — check out information yourself.

2. Don't think your teen is going to be the exception. "My son would never ..." The truth is that, "Yes, he would" and he probably already has.

3. Snoop around — listen to conversations kids are having when they don't think you are listening, but only when you have "probable cause," such as a phone call from a fellow parent or a strong, intuitive sense that "something is up."

4. Talk to your teen frequently about the dangers of drinking, smoking, drug use, etc. You may not think he is listening, but somewhere in there, he is.

5. Give stringent consequences for violations. Impose a shorter leash on activities.

6. Try to have conversations about choice and consequences — yelling will just alienate and turn him off.

7. Don't share stories about your drinking/drug days. Don't assume that because you did, he will or because you didn't, he won't. Anything is possible.

8. Remind him that the legal drinking age is 21 and so the biggest reason not to drink is because it is illegal. Don't be afraid to tell your teen it scares you to think of him drinking/using drugs and don't be afraid to let him know where you stand on alcohol use/abuse.

9. Examine your own alcohol use and make sure your own drinking isn't contributing to any problem your teen might be having.

2. To Drink or Not to Drink

I recently had a discussion with 17-year-old Michael about drinking. He was driving me to the airport as I was going on a five-day vacation with four of my friends from high school. It was actually a good time to bring up "touchy" subjects. Whenever I go away on trips, Michael gets nervous about the possibility of my dying.

This harkens back to a time when he was seven-years-old and a number of female relatives and friends died rather suddenly, including his grandmother and aunt. Since that time, he has always had a fear that I could suddenly die — and this fear becomes exaggerated on those few occasions when I fly somewhere.

At those times, Michael always wants me to know how much he loves me and what a special mom I am. I always reciprocate and tell him how proud I am of him and what a great person he is and how dearly I love him. Then I tell him I know how he worries when I go away that something bad might happen to me. While I know that's a possibility, I tell him that it also is rather unlikely and to please not worry. He then begins to ask questions about where I'm going and what I'll be doing when I get there. I proceed to tell him — I'm going to Carmel, California with five of my high school friends — our yearly trip — and how we like to take side trips, for instance going to Sonoma Valley for a winery tour. He's interested in this, wanting to know if we get to taste any wine.

My ears now begin to perk up, as I see this as a perfect opportunity to probe around the drinking arena. So I tell him "Yes, part of the tour includes tasting because the wineries want you to buy their wine." So then I ask him, trying to sound mater of fact, "Do you like wine?" He shakes his head "Na, hate the taste."

"How about hard liquor?" I risk asking.

"Nope — hate it," he replies.

I'm liking this "getting info" conversation, I must say, and it's pretty easy — so far. Let's push a little further. "Well, what do you like — what's your favorite — beer?"

"Yep — I like beer."

"Do you love it?" I'm digging now and I know it, but hey, he's afraid I might die, so I might as well keep asking. God only knows he's not going to get mad at me because he's afraid he might never see me again, — so let's push again.

"What do you mean, do I love it?" he asks suspiciously. I know by the sound of his voice that I'm pushing a little too much and, of course, I am. But having lived with an alcoholic father and sister, I know that loving alcohol of any kind is dangerous — at least in my experience. So I push on, but with a slight degree of caution.

"Oh, you know," I say, "when you can't wait until the weekend because then you'll be able to drink and you spend a lot of time thinking about it during the week — in anticipation."

There, I said it.

He then looks at me, with one eye cocked and says, "Mom, I am not an alcoholic. I enjoy drinking a beer or two — not ten — not a case — and, no, I don't think about it all week. Will you please stop worrying. I am not an alcoholic — did you hear that?"

"OK — OK," I say. "You can't blame me for asking. It's part of my job as a parent and also part of my paranoia as a child of an alcoholic. So you have to cut me some slack."

"I know," he says "but you can't keep asking me. You really have to trust what I'm telling you."

I know he's right and I am reassured — for now. Like Michael and how his fear of my dying requires reassurance from me — my fear of him becoming an alcoholic requires reassurance from him. So, for now, both of us have been reassured around our fears and both of us are O.K.

TOOLS USED

1. Pick a time for serious talk when you are doing something else. Driving in the car can be a great opportunity because you're not looking directly at each other. For some

reason, this activates the door to more communication between parents and teens. Orchestrating reasons to be in the car together or running errands together frequently is one way to connect with your teen. Try it!

2. Ask questions about drinking. Ask about his views on drinking. Try to make the conversation casual, not accusatory.

3. Ask information about how and when your teen drinks. He will probably resist this, but ask anyway.

4. Use the time to teach about drinking and drugs as well as to ask questions about it. This may require that you get accurate information yourself about what constitutes alcohol/drug abuse vs. alcoholism/ drug addiction.

5. Talk about any family history of drinking or drug problems and how that can impact on your teen; i.e. being in the "wrong" gene pool.

3. Smoking

I hate that my 17-year-old smokes — although he frequently reminds me that it's only "once in a while." I don't like that he does it at all — ever. I have only one view of it and that view is "It's stupid, stupid, stupid." It's one bad thing that you can absolutely make a decision to say "No" to — and be certain that that decision is doing a tremendous service to your body.

I am admittedly irrational and one-sided on the subject and completely unapologetic about it. Every chance I get, I ply Michael with information, particularly about the effects of second-hand smoke.

I first became suspicious as I was doing laundry. Michael's clothes smelled to high heaven of smoke. At the time I just assumed his friends must be smoking and it really never occurred to me that Michael would be. Neither I nor his dad smoke and we don't allow anyone to smoke in our home. We have always been anti-smoking, although not the poster-carrying, Bible thumping, in your face kind of believers. Just the usual "Don't like smoke" — don't like it in my hair or on my clothes or in my throat, in my home kind of people, so we just avoid places where smoking is allowed. Never occurred to either of us that our children would ever even consider smoking, much less do it on any regular basis. We figured there is simply too much evidence out there for anyone to start the habit anymore — unless they were stupid.

Well, I guess we were wrong — not about the stupid part, but about the "who could ever start smoking with all the evidence there is against it?" part. Denial is a powerful defense and teenagers are full of it. At least mine is.

I was stunned to learn from Michael that I should be glad he only smokes once in a while since he used to smoke regularly. "Regularly" I say, stunned even more. "When, regularly? You're only 16."

"When I was in 8th grade, and freshman year in high school," he says.

"You're kidding," I say. Where was I, I want to know? How could my kid be smoking regularly and I not know it? How could I miss the clues or, better yet, what did I do with the clues I had? This was definitely another lesson in humility. I, who pride myself on my keen intuition, insight, and ability to sniff out problems or inklings of problems before they get big — how could I have missed this?

The only way I can answer that is to say it must have been denial — or refusal. As I look back, I do remember the smoky-smelling clothes, but I rationalized them by telling myself that I knew some of his friends smoked, so it must be from them — it couldn't be from Michael. I truly did not let that possibility enter my brain. Just never went there.

And I think the clincher was smelling smoke in his car and, whenever he used the family car, smelling it in there. I then went to him, angrily and said: "What's up with the smoke smell in the cars? You know it's a house rule that there is no smoking in any of the cars — period — the end. Not negotiable."

Michael then proceeded to say that no one would drive in his car with him if he didn't allow the smokers to smoke. So I started asking more questions, like, "How frequently are people smoking and frankly, if they're smoking, you must be smoking, too."

To be honest, I think I threw that in assuming he would say, "No, I don't smoke" but that's not what he said. Instead, he replied, "I only smoke once in a while." I then flew off into lecture mode, saying things like "I can't believe you would pick up a cigarette knowing all you do about its dangers. How could you? It's a stupid decision and besides, you're an athlete — how stupid is that?" I'm sure I said more, not as rationally as I thought, but suffice it to say I let my disappointment and anger come pouring out. I think what bothers me most about it is the lack of control I have over stopping him. And, because I can't really do anything about it, I erroneously feel if I give him enough information about it, he won't smoke at all. I'm still trying to control from the sidelines. And I'm thinking that it's not working. How do I know that? I know that by the look on Michael's face every time I descend upon him with another article or NPR show or cancer story — he immediately rolls his eyes and says something like "Here she goes again."

So, when am I going to get it? When am I going to stop badgering him about this? I'll tell you when that time will come — it will never come. Oh yes, I'm learning to back off a little and Michael does tell me that he smokes so little that all the energy I'm spending on lecturing isn't worth it — he's tuning it out anyway. So, maybe my job needs to be one of quiet disapproval, or disgusting looks when I take his smelly clothes from his room, or I can hold my nose whenever I get in his car — I can do any and all of those things, but how mature is that? And frankly, around this issue, I'm not so sure how mature I want to be. I'll keep harping and singing the "No Smoking" song until he stops — and I have no clue how long that will be.

TOOL USED

1. Give your teen information about the horrors of smoking even though you know it may not be enough to stop him from doing it.

2. Tell him you disapprove of it and want him to stop.

3. Tell him regularly.

4. Offer incentives for stopping — in our case, it was being able to use one of our cars exclusively for his own use.

5. Plaster "No Smoking" signs all over.

6. Talk about the power of denial.

7. Set up consequences if your teen continues to smoke.

8. Talk about your disappointment in him for doing something that can have such long-term negative impact on his health.

9. Look at your own behavior. If you smoke, know that your credibility with your teen is pretty nonexistent. If you're going to ask your teen to stop smoking, you should be willing to stop smoking yourself — do it together!

4. The First Brush with the Law

It was 7:30 a.m. and 17-year-old Andrew was gone. He and his two friends had checked in at 12:30 am to say they were in for the night and, as usual, they would be sleeping in the basement. OK — fine. So, when I went downstairs the following morning to put a load of laundry in and saw no one sleeping on the couches, I was totally surprised — how could that be? Where could they have gone? It was certainly too early for them to have gotten up and gone for something to eat — it was, after all, 7:30 a.m., not p.m.. So, where in the heck were they?

I searched everywhere in the house and finally looked outside. All the cars were there. So, if they weren't in the house and all the cars were here, where could they have possibly gone? I called all of their cell phones and got only voice mail. Very unusual. All of this was very unusual. So what to do? I called Tom and he had no idea that they weren't home when he went off to work. So we decided I would do more detective work and call him if there was cause for concern.

What to do next? What I didn't want to do was to flip out or panic. I needed to keep my wits about me. Plus, I kept thinking that no news was probably good news. I did, though, turn on the local news channel to make sure they weren't part of a "breaking news" story. Relieved that they weren't, I began to go through the litany of possibilities: 1. They could have gone down the street to our neighbor's house and fallen asleep there. I get hopeful about that possibility and call my friend — no, she hadn't seen them; 2. One of Andrew's friends could have picked them all up and taken them to someone else's house. That's never happened before, but it is a possibility. I call a few of Andrew's friends and no one has seen any of the boys since last night; 3. They could be dead somewhere. Possible, but not probable. Since I had already turned on the TV and nothing was mentioned on the news, I had to believe this was not the most likely scenario.

At this point, I was running out of obvious possibilities and could feel my blood pressure beginning to rise and panic making its move inside. It was at this precise moment that my cell phone rang — it was Andrew. Immediately, I could feel my body relax and I took a breath that said, "OK, he's alive — I don't have to be scared. Now I can afford to be mad."

"Uh, Ma," he says, drawing out the "ah" sound. I know that tone of voice — it always means he's done something he shouldn't. And had gotten caught.

"Where are you?" I ask.

"Uh, at the police station," he says.

"The police station!" I yell, "Whatever for?"

"Well, we uh, kind of got arrested last night."

Then the story comes out. They decided, in all their wisdom, to go outside at 1:00 a.m. when they saw it was snowing outside. They began to throw snowballs at cars pulling up to the stop sign at our corner. Then they would run away. Apparently, one or two of the motorists called the police and the boys were caught. With alcohol in a backpack, no less. And when they were arrested, they were not allowed to make any phone calls. Instead, they were taken down to the police station, photographed, fingerprinted, and put in a holding cell until morning. They were just being released and could I come and pick them up?

"No way!" I say. "I'm so mad at you, I don't want to see you for awhile. Walk home and then we'll talk about this. In the meantime, I will be contacting the other boys' parents."

So, while the jailbirds were walking home, I call the other teens' homes to inform them of the "arrest." One boy's parents must be at work — no answer. The other boy's parents are home; they are mortified, and the dad will come to pick up his son. He arrives just before the boys do. We laugh a bit at their combined stupidity and with relief that nothing bad happened as a result of their actions. We then discuss our strategy. It's simple: Lecture. Guilt inducement. Consequences.

The boys come in looking very guilty, scared and apologetic. Good sign. Already I think they have learned an important lesson. Then the other teen's dad and I proceeded to lecture from a variety of perspectives:

Nothing good happens after midnight.

Drinking in a group leads to stupid and often dangerous behavior.

They violated our trust by checking in and then leaving the house.

We were scared not knowing where they were or what had happened to them.

Although they saw throwing snowballs as "fun," especially after drinking, they could have injured a motorist or caused an accident or even someone's death.

They now had an arrest record. This would have to be expunged which would be an expense to us as parents.

They had a court date, which could mean hiring an attorney.

They would now have consequences to deal with, to be determined by each teen's parents.

The boys were very apologetic, seemed to grasp some of the severity of what they had done, but were probably most upset by the fact that they knew they would be grounded for a period of time — which they were.

What was good about the experience was that each set of parents was on the same page regarding the need for consequences and each determined the level of punishment for their own teen.

We all went to court on the allotted day and the case was dismissed for a variety of reasons. What seemed very apparent was the fact that the officers wanted to teach the kids a lesson — which they did. It was good for the boys to have to sit in court, get treated like criminals, be scared of what might happen, and evaluate whether a few thrown snowballs, after having a few beers was worth all the time, energy, effort, money, consequences and embarrassment that resulted from one act of stupidity.

TOOLS USED

1. Try not to go to the "worst case scenario" right at the beginning. Don't let panic rule you.

2. Figure out possible logical scenarios and follow them through before moving to scarier scenarios.

3. When you finally find your teen, get his story about what happened before you get mad.

4. Help him understand all of the possible outcomes that "could have happened."

5. Help him understand the severity of what he did.

6. Tell him how disappointed you are and how his behavior violated your trust

7. Give your teen consequences for his behavior and follow through. Also be mindful that the consequences you give your son may be different from another parent's. That's OK.

8. Make him pay for any expenses you incur as a result of his behavior.

9. Let him know how frightening it was for you to not know where he was.

10. Let the other parents know how you have decided to handle the situation and why. It helps to share perspectives, even if you don't agree on outcome.

CHAPTER 10

Parties
and Sleepovers

1. Parties

When I think of teenage parties, a number of images and thoughts come into my head — things like: big parties with lots of kids, lots of drinking and not an adult in sight; kids showing up at someone's home when they know the parents are out of town; having an impromptu party that gets out of hand; backyard barbeques with lots of kids just eating, drinking pop and having fun — with parents in the house. Anyway I think of it, however, the operative words are "lots of kids."

Lots of kids can be lots of fun or lots of trouble — there's a very thin line that separates the two. As a parent, I feel like I'm almost always playing some level of detective. I try not to make my "checking things out" turn into an interrogation session. I like to think that I operate, to a large degree, on the premise of trusting my teen until such time as I have a reason not to. But, in reality, I don't think that's true. And if you ask my kids, they don't think so either. They think I'm basically paranoid and worry too much. I think they're right — and I also think that's basically my parenting style — for the good and bad of it. I want to know who you're with, where you are going and what you are doing. If you are at a friend's house and there's a party, I want to know if a parent is present and I want to talk to that parent.

Of course, I'm not naive enough to think my older son doesn't go to some parties where there is no supervision and simply doesn't tell me. I just hope that (on some level) he remembers all of those lectures given ad nauseum by his father and me about the dangers of "runaway parties" and how when drinking, no supervision and groups of teenagers are combined, trouble usually follows. And, we constantly remind him, as an athlete in a varsity sport, one stupid act can definitely blow a season of play.

I guess when I think of it, our basic approach is to teach our children to think through their choices before they make them, so they can anticipate trouble or problems. Of course, I also think

I can still choose better than they can and would, if they would only consult me more often than they do!

I must also say I am heartened every time I hear an example from them where they exercised good judgment. For instance, when Michael was 16 he had to leave our family vacation three days early so he could participate in varsity volleyball. Not being at practice would have resulted in him not being on the team. So, we allowed him to go home early as long as he agreed to have his grandmother stay with him on the nights he was home alone. He reluctantly agreed, saying he didn't like it because he could handle being alone, and why didn't we trust him, but if that was the only way he could come home early, he'd do it.

Well, wouldn't you know, on the second night he was home, a group of teenagers from his school (who weren't, by the way, his usual group of friends) showed up at the house, toting a case of beer, saying they heard Michael was having a party. To Michael's credit, he told them he was not having a party and to get the hell out with the beer. Hawkeye Grandma was not far behind, yelling at them to get their butts and their beer out of the house!

Now who knows if he would have had the same reaction had Hawkeye Grandma not been around, but I suppose that is precisely the point. There's no reason for him to be in the position of having to chase kids away because there's no adult around. At least with an adult present, your teen can blame the adult for ruining a good time. He does not have to decide, on the spot, if he can stand up to his peers. I guess this keeps pointing out to me how important it is for us to be around when they are, just in case ...

TOOLS USED

1. Know that teens do make a habit of looking for parties, especially unsupervised ones. Keep your ears open.

2. Always ask where your teen is, who he is with and if there is an adult present. Ask regularly. Don't hesitate to call the home where your teen is visiting and ask to speak to the parent.

3. Trust your instincts. If you have a "funny feeling" that something is not right, it probably isn't. Check it out.

4. If you are going to leave your teen at home alone, check on him regularly or have a friend, neighbor or relative make a "teen check."

2. The Unsupervised Party

He wanted to have a "few" friends over to play cards while we, his parents, were going to be away on vacation. "No big deal — it's only a few people and it's just to play cards. Don't worry, mom. It'll be fine. I promise." Right!

I should have listened to my husband who said, "Let's say no. We have no idea who might show up and what it might turn into. We'll be far away with no way to check anything out." I say, "I think we can trust him. If he says it'll only be a few kids, it'll only be a few kids. I say we give him a chance."

"Ok," says Tom, "but I have to tell you, I don't feel good about it."

Fast forward to the day after the "I'm only having a few friends over" non-party. Michael calls us to "see how we're doing" and begins to hem and haw, obviously hesitating around saying something. We ask him what's wrong and he wants to know if there's something "peculiar" about the sliding glass back door. "What do you mean?" I ask. "Well, somehow the back door was knocked off its hinges and I got it back on track, but it won't lock — the lock's broken."

After a number of detailed questions, it finally comes out that Michael actually had a full-fledged party — beer keg and all! — and someone "accidently" ran into the back door. "Did anything else "accidently" happen and did that "accident" happen as the result of somebody drinking?"

Michael hedges in his answers, which, of course, in itself, is very telling. He says that the door was the only broken thing, but that he's never having another party because "it's too much work and too much monitoring."

"Too much work — too much monitoring?" I say, "How many kids did you have? And be honest with me because you know I'll find out anyway, so you might as well fess up." He hems and haws again and finally says, "Only about 40 kids and they weren't loud and nothing bad happened, so don't get mad at me, OK? I was really responsible during the whole thing!"

What an oxymoron that was! How could he be "responsible" when he wasn't supposed to have a party in the first place? The way I saw it, he was "responsible" for being deceptive and sneaky — for lying by omission. He, of course, said it was something that "just sort of happened" rather than something that was planned.

Sorry — you don't end up with a keg of beer without planning it ahead of time! Conclusion — our son lied to us!

Well, when we got home, Tom and I took a walk through the house to assess any additional, previously unmentioned-by-Michael, damage. The house was pretty clean, I must admit, although not exactly up to my standard, nor in the condition in which I left it prior to vacation. I did get some pleasure, however, from observing how good Michael had been with "clean-up." He did learn that lesson well! However, that pleasure was soon eclipsed by annoyance when I saw a punched hole in one of the basement doors — another obvious tribute to the aftermath of teenage drinking without supervision.

Add to that a conversation I had with a neighbor who had

"checked" on the party and said it "wasn't too loud" and the kids were respectful, but they had started a wood fire in the yard using gasoline as starter fluid! All I could do was grab my heart, shake my head and feel grateful that nothing worse than two broken doors had occurred. At least I had a house to come home to! How pathetic is that when you end up feeling "grateful" that you only have "minor" damage to your home after a party that wasn't supposed to have happened in the first place?! I was certainly glad the house was still standing, but very disappointed that, just when I think my son has passed the threshold into adult maturity, he does something that makes me shake my head. I had to remind myself that he was still only 18-years-old and still learning how to negotiate the difference between how he "thinks" something is going to turn out from how it actually turns out.

So, as a result of this "non-party," Michael learned he doesn't want to do another large party because it was more work than it was worth and we learned (or "I" learned) not to leave an 18-year-old home alone over a weekend and expect that he won't do something I'll be sorry for at the end of it. Next time, "Hawkeye" Grandma will be staying with any teenager left behind at our house!

TOOLS USED

1. Don't leave a teenager home alone while you go off on vacation, even if you think you can trust him. You may be able to trust him, but other people can show up and make the job impossible for a teen.

2. Make your teen pay for any damages that occurred. In our case, we took money from Michael's account to cover the cost of a new lock and fixing the hole in the door. If he doesn't have an account, make him work it off.

3. Talk with your teen about the consequences of his actions and how what he thought would happen doesn't always resemble what, in fact, does happen.

4. Talk about what happens when a large group of unsupervised, drinking teenagers get together and how control over a situation can quickly be lost, no matter what your intentions are.

5. Talk about your own disappointment in your teenager for having taken your trust and violated it and your feelings about that.

6. Decide whether or not additional punishment is needed such as grounding, working around the house, loss of driving privileges, no friends for a period of time or writing about what he learned from this experience.

3. Eavesdropping

The opportunity came up rather suddenly and I had to decide quickly whether I would or I wouldn't. I decided I would. Eavesdrop that is — on my older son. Initially I felt a little "slimy" about it, but the more I listened the more I was glad I had decided to listen in.

What prompted this, you might ask? And is this something I did regularly? No, I almost never do it, but this time I was prompted by a series of comments and activities Michael was engaging in all through the weekend. It seemed like he was on the phone nonstop, with a number of people, carrying on alternately very heated or very frustrating, lengthy discussions. Lengthy for him and his friends. And, when I would comment about any of this, he would only say something cryptic like, "God, there's a lot of drama going on" followed by some frustrating or exasperated sound.

When I asked him to elaborate, he would only say something like "Never mind — it's too complicated to explain." And I would say something like "OK, if you want to talk about it, I'm happy to listen." What I was thinking, however, was "God I'd like to be a fly on the wall and know what's going on ... Tell me, so I can help you."

But I restrained myself and, I must say, it was very hard to do. So, when an opportunity arose when Michael answered the kitchen phone — which, gratefully, was not a cordless phone — I decided to tune in. He could only walk into his brother's room, which is right off of the kitchen, to have his conversation. And since he left the door open, I decided this would be the perfect time to get some things done in the kitchen.

Would it really be eavesdropping if I just happened to overhear him talking in the next room? After all, I didn't have my ear to the door or anything. I was just going about my business in the kitchen and couldn't help but overhear his conversation. This is how I gave myself permission to quench my curiosity — and I'm glad I did because I learned a lot.

What I heard made me proud. I heard my son act like a mature and caring adult. The conversation he was having was with a girl he had asked to the homecoming dance. He was telling her that he was really sorry and he didn't want to hurt her feelings, but that he had been realizing this week how uncomfortable he was every time he thought about this dance. And what he concluded was that he knew this girl liked him more than he liked her and maybe they shouldn't go because it meant more to her than it did to him. He also made statements like "When I thought about you, I realized that I don't really know you very well — I've never seen your house or met your parents — I really don't know you very well at all and I don't think going to this dance is the way to get to know you better. It's too much pressure."

I could tell from his end of the conversation that this must have been a great relief to the girl, because Michael's side was one of relief as well. It sounded as though the feelings were mutual. They agreed to cancel the dance and left it by agreeing to be friends but not date.

I was very impressed with how Michael handled himself — his willingness to pay attention to his discomfort, to talk to this girl about it and come to a resolution that worked for both of them — all of this without any help from me or his Dad. It felt good to know that I had overheard something that was very reassuring and encouraging to me. Reassuring in that Michael could make good decisions on his own — that he could be strong enough to know when he had made a mistake and be able to correct it — himself. It was encouraging because I knew that in a year he would be off on his own — in college — and that the judgment I heard him exercise in this situation reflected a strength of character that will be with him his entire lifetime. And as far as eavesdropping is concerned, I'm not feeling the need to do that on a regular basis, but I do reserve the right to use it when I think my child's behavior warrants it. You never know what you are going to hear.

TOOLS USED

1. Listen to your teen's conversations when you pick up that something "troubling" is going on that might require intervention. If, during the course of listening you decide intervention will not be needed, stop listening!

2. Reserve eavesdropping for true concerns you have about your teenager. Don't use it indiscriminately.

3. If you decide intervention is necessary, let your teen know the reasons why you decided to eavesdrop. Talk about your concerns with him.

4. Sleepovers — as in Co-Ed

He didn't think it was a big deal — didn't want to worry me — was exercising good judgment. These were all the reasons my 17-year-old gave for not informing us that two of his "girl" friends had spent the night at our house.

We discovered it by accident. All of our teenager's sleepovers happen in the basement. My 14-year-old son Andrew was having two friends overnight. Michael had called at 11:30 p.m. and asked if his three friends could sleep over. "Fine" I said. I knew both groups would get along fine and there's certainly enough room for everyone. I just told Michael to check in with us when he got home, which he did. He came in around 1:15 a.m. to let us know he and his friends were home. We actually chatted for about 15 minutes. His Dad and I had just attended a "back to school" night where we met all of his teachers, so Michael was very curious to know what we thought. We talked about how impressed I was with the level of knowledge and devotion his teachers displayed and how fortunate I thought he was to have them. He went on to elaborate on his own thoughts and feelings about his teachers and I was delighted we had had this extended conversation, especially since it was 1:40 in the morning.

During all of this wonderful bonding experience, however, Michael failed to tell me that two girls were also in the basement and would be sleeping over. This fact was not discovered until late the next morning when Tom went into the basement to get something and noticed a purse with a bra sticking out of it on the floor outside of Michael's bedroom. And Michael was not in his room, but sleeping on the floor in another part of the basement. Michael must have heard Tom, because he told him "By the way, Dad, two of the girls spent the night. Don't worry — nothing happened — they're in my bedroom with the door locked. It was too late to drive them home, so I told them to stay over."

Tom promptly runs up to tell me so we could discuss what to

do. My first reaction was one of being mortified, then angry. Here Michael and I had had this really nice conversation the night before and he neglects to tell me this critical piece of information that he knows is important for us to know.

We call Michael up from the basement to talk about it. He comes up looking apologetic, so we already know that he knows he did something he shouldn't have. He proceeds to give his lame excuses and we proceed to tell him that had he told us, we probably would have let the girls stay, but would have put them on another floor — or we would have taken them home ourselves. What we objected strongly to was not being informed. Also, Andrew had two new friends staying overnight, and our concern was that they would go home and tell their parents that the Brennans had a co-ed sleep over — not a good thing!

So, Michael got the point — apologized again — but this incident did leave us with the firm belief that Michael still needs some more lessons on thinking through his choices and we need to keep our vigilance around asking questions and checking up on our kids and checking out our assumptions.

As I reflect on this a little more, I'm also aware of how differently I dealt with this than I would have three years ago. For one thing, I wasn't as flipped out — for another, neither were they. I think part of the reason for this is that teenagers nowadays tend to hang out in "packs" and aren't necessarily paired off like they were "in my day." Also, neither of these girls was Michael's "girlfriend" — they are his friends, so I wasn't as worried about him having a sex orgy right under my very nose. However, I'm also aware of how slippery this can be and the importance of learning how to keep "safe" boundaries — this is where an ounce of prevention is worth a pound of cure!

TOOLS USED

1. Ask your teen exactly who is sleeping over in your home.

2.   Check for yourself on the sleeping arrangements once the kids are settled in.

3.   Explain ahead of time to your teen what the rules are regarding sleepovers and what the consequences are, should the rules be violated.

5. The "Surprise" Party

I thought that perhaps we would bypass this with our second child. Erroneously, I believed that 14-year-old Andrew would skip into teenagedom and not suffer from some of the same issues we had already handled with his older brother. Apparently not. Apparently repetition or learning from one's own mistakes ranks higher in "teendom" than learning from the mistakes of others. So, what was the lesson, you might ask?

The lesson was: Do not have friends over when your parents are not home and do not, absolutely do not, tell some of those friends that your parents are not home, because faster than you can say "lickety split," you will have the beginnings or middles of a party at your house.

It started out tamely enough. Tom and I were going to our older son's Varsity basketball game an hour away from home. Andrew opted not to go, instead asking if he could have "a few" friends over after he finished studying. We agreed. During our time away, we checked in with Andrew and all was well. He had four friends over and they were playing Nintendo on T.V. Fine. An hour later, as we are driving home from the game, Andrew calls. He's sounding a little frantic. Says "a bunch of kids" showed up at the house — uninvited — and he wanted to know what he should do. I asked him how many kids — he said about thirty. Thirty! I said he had to tell them to leave because there was not a parent in the house. I also told him to tell the group that we would call the police if they didn't leave. He said he would do that. I felt anxious and wished that we were closer to the house than we were.

We arrived home about twenty minutes later to the following scene: One parent had just pulled up to pick up four of the girls. Seven or eight boys and girls were just starting to leave the house through the garage door; several other kids were hanging out by the alley and, as we walked into the basement, there were about 20 boys and girls spread out all over the basement. My immediate reaction was surprise and annoyance. Andrew came up at that point and said he told the kids to leave and they did go outside, but then someone else let them back in and he had been trying to get them out ever since.

Some of the kids were "schmoozing" just a little too much — too much politeness and too many questions about the basket-ball game. I became increasingly suspicious of them and was sure some of them had been drinking. I told the whole crew they had to go home and to start arranging rides. They were quite accom-modating at this point because they knew we were mad.

Then I started sleuthing around the house, smelling pop cans, looking for the hard evidence that my instincts told me had to be around somewhere. Spotted a small thermos bottle on the table — picked it up — smelled it — no smell — tasted it — ick! The mouth awakening taste of straight vodka!

By this time some of the kids had already been picked up. About half of the crew was left waiting outside. Talked with Tom about what to do — decided to confront them with the evidence. Asked Andrew first if he knew anything about it — he denied it. The thermos was pink and purple, a pretty sure sign that it be-longed to one of the girls.

We went outside and asked if anyone was willing to admit ownership of this thermos — predictably, there were no takers. Proceeded to tell them there was vodka in it and that first of all, they were too young to be drinking. Secondly, we wanted them to know that we really wanted our house to be a welcoming house, but at our house we would not allow drinking, nor would we allow kids who had been drinking in our home. Reminded them they were only 14-years-old and we were doing what each one of their parents would do if they were in our shoes. The kids were mostly silent, then apologetic, although not directly admitting to any wrongdoing. Told them to come back in the house and wait for their rides — which they did.

We spoke with Andrew after everyone had left, asking him what he had learned from this. He said two things: 1) Don't tell friends your parents aren't home; 2) Don't let large numbers of kids in the house — especially drinking kids — because things can get out of hand quickly. Andrew had been unnerved because kids wouldn't listen to him and he didn't know what to do. He knew they had been drinking once they came in, but part of the problem was that they kept coming — due to the miracle of cell phones, and he was out of his league. It was lucky we got home when we did to interrupt what would have been a continuation of partying.

We decided not to call everyone's parents, in part because we didn't know most of the kids and we didn't know who was drinking and who wasn't. Perhaps that was a mistake — I'm not quite sure. I was approached the next morning by the mother of one of the kids who apologized for not having found out whether a parent was going to be home before letting her son come over. She complimented Andrew on having told the kids to leave the house and was sorry her son contributed to the chaos of the evening. I did report the rest of the details to her and she was also very disappointed, saying that "this part" of being a teenager had begun now for them as well.

So, the big lesson here is that vigilance, asking questions and checking up on your teen on a regular basis is the order of the day.

TOOLS USED

1. Be sure you know where your teenager is and who he is with — particularly on the weekends.

2. If he is at a friend's house, talk to a parent to make sure there is adult supervision in the house.

3. Have your teen check in with you regularly during the evening.

4. Don't let him simply "roam" around the neighborhood — particularly if he is in a group larger than four.

5. Make sure he has a destination and that he lets you know when he has arrived and when he is leaving for the next destination.

6. Expect your teen's planning to be last minute as well as unclear. Press for clarity. This helps him, too.

7. If kids are in your home, particularly if they are in your basement, find reasons to go down and check on them.

8. Trust your intuition. If you feel like they are "up" to something, they probably are. Stay vigilant.

9. Ask questions — frequently. Ask if he is doing something he shouldn't and caution him to think through to the consequences of his behavior.

10. Congratulate him when he does show good judgement, good behavior and/or makes good choices.

11. Let him know that you start out trusting him and you hope he doesn't violate that trust. If he does, then the rules change. There will be more of them.

12. Keep your eyes and ears open.

13. Be around when he is.

6. Graduation Party Dilemma

It should have been a "slam-dunk" decision but it wasn't. It should have been clear that the answer would simply be "No Way!" But that wasn't the way it happened. Nope. Instead, it happened this way ...

We were planning Michael's high school graduation party and looking forward to celebrating this important milestone with and for him. From our perspective, it would be a straightforward kind of party — family, friends and neighbors plus Michael's friends — weather permitting, in the yard — lots of food, low-key fun. But then Michael threw in the loaded question, "Can my friends and I drink "a little" at my party?"

"No way," we say and decide that's the end of that discussion — there WILL be no discussion.

But, persistent child that he is, Michael begins to hammer — not belligerently, mind you. No. He hammers with teen-age logic. The logic that says "When I drink, I drink responsibly and so do my friends. If anyone gets out of line, there's always one of us around to keep order." He insists that he will be able to keep his friends in control — that it's only one night, it's his graduation party; he's going away soon and won't have us watching over him, so why not practice now? The big argument, however, was that he had already been to a number of graduation parties where parents allowed the kids to drink. The parents told the kids that they would have to agree there would be no drinking and driving. They were to have a designated driver or spend the night at the party house. They could drink as long as they agreed to those rules plus they had to stay in the house or in the yard. And, Michael added, the police showed up at two of the parties and just told them to keep the noise down. In Michael's mind, all of this added up to permission to do the same thing at our house.

Now, I must admit to have been somewhat taken in by this logic. It implies that "everyone is doing it." By allowing drinking in the controlled environment of your own home, you're actually preventing some danger because the kids will be drinking anyway. Following that logic, why not allow it where you can keep them safer rather than have them roaming around somewhere and perhaps getting into more trouble?

Of course, all of this "logic" avoids the more basic issue: it is illegal to begin with. Add to that the extreme personal liability should anyone get out of our imposed "safety net" and either hurt themselves or someone else.

Ultimately, we landed on the spot we started on — "No!" But, I must admit, it was a bit of a struggle to get there. A struggle, in part, because we want our son to have a good time at his own party. We want his friends to have a good time as well. We also struggled because other parents, whom we like and respect, allowed teen drinking in their homes and nothing bad happened, so should we go along with them or stick to our guns?

What it finally came down to for us, though, were two principles: 1) Allowing underage drinking inside our home would be doing something outside of OUR integrity. It would be compromising around an issue that did not feel like a compromise as much as it felt like a capitulation to our son feeling good about it and his friends thinking we were "cool;" and, 2) We were unwilling to jeopardize our reputations and our financial holdings over the possibility that one of these 18-year-olds could hurt themselves or someone else as a direct result of being at our party. It would simply not be worth the vigilance and stress we would live with — and for what? To allow kids to get drunk at our house so they would like us better? What WERE we thinking?

I am glad and relieved that we eventually came to our senses and gave a definitive "No." This, after at least two weeks of back-and-forth discussions, examining this issue from every conceivable angle and feeling a myriad of ways about it emotionally, spiritually and practically. And it did make us sad as well — sad to think that "fun" for our son and his friends often includes drinking as a necessary component. Sad that we thought we had raised Michael in a way that would make him so aware of the alcoholic gene pool he came from that he would stay as far away from alcohol as he could. But that's not the case. While we think he is very aware of his genetics, he is certainly choosing to find his own drinking level, so to speak. We just hope that it doesn't reach over the line into any addiction. Instead, we hope he is able to determine his "safe" drinking use. We're just sorry that he is accepting the risks that underage drinking carries with it. I am glad, however, that at least we, as parents, decided not to join him there.

TOOLS USED

1. Begin the conversation about graduation parties long before the season begins.

2. Let your son know your philosophy regarding drinking at these parties.

3. Beware that you might feel yourself being tempted into wanting to be a "cool" parent or wanting to control where the graduates drink, thereby letting them drink under your supervision. Don't do it.

4. Underage drinking is illegal — period. Whether you agree or disagree, it's the law and you, as a parent, could suffer legal consequences should you allow drinking in your home.

5. Use your decision to teach your teen, once again, that although you're making a decision that is unpopular, you are acting from integrity and you expect the same behavior from him — even if it's hard.

CHAPTER 11

In School
and
After School

1. Grades

My 14-year-old, Andrew, who just started high school, came home announcing that his first progress reports would be coming home soon. "Is there something we should know or be concerned about?" I asked.

"No, I don't think so" he replied. "But I'm not sure."

"Elaborate on that," I suggest.

But Andrew is not really a detail kind of kid. He likes to give "broad brush" answers and doesn't like to be prodded or nibbled with questions. So, I always end up trying to decide how much quizzing it's safe to do. In this instance, I decided to try the "broad" approach. "Well," I said, "how do you think you are doing?"

"O.K." he says. "I'm probably only getting one or two A's and the rest B's — maybe one C, so don't get mad about it — remember, it's only my first quarter and it's only a progress report."

Well, I think, what he's telling me is fine — if he's getting mostly A's and B's and maybe one C — that's great — isn't it? Yes, I think — yes, it is — BUT — and the but ends up being pretty big, — but, I know that these grades are not his best. I have to bite my tongue (very hard, mind you) not to say that. Especially when I would also like to add that his older brother, who has a learning disability, has gotten straight A's and two B's his entire high school career. And has had to work twice as hard to get it!

But, no, I don't say that. Instead I say, "How would you rate your effort this quarter?" and he says, "I'd give myself an A-. Why, how would you rate me?"

I know this could be tricky, but decide to tell the truth. "Based on the amount of time I've seen you study versus the time you spend watching TV or being with friends, I'd give you a B and Dad gives you a B+. So, do I need to give you the "Are you doing your very best" lecture?

"No" Andrew replies. "I know what I have to do and I will do it — I don't want to hear any lecture about it — that'll just make me mad."

"O.K." I say "Enough said." And I walk away. But all the time I'm walking away, I'm biting my tongue because I know that magical, life-changing, light bulb-making, do your best lecture that is aching to jump out of my mouth will have to be put away for another day and I do know that day will come — it just won't be today. Today I have to trust that my son is taking responsibility for his own road to success and that he really doesn't need me to remind him of what he already knows. I am, however, just aching to tell him anyway.

TOOLS USED

1. Decide together with your teen what your expectations are regarding grades. In our case, the expectation is "your best" and "C's" don't come within the realm of Andrew's best. If he can do better, he should. After all, being a student is his full time job. He should do his best.

2. Ask your teen how he is doing in school. Give him the opportunity to inform you.

3. As long as your teen is performing according to your agreement, let him be in charge of managing his time and homework.

4. If the agreement is broken, your teen is no longer in charge of his time management. You are. Make that clear at the beginning of the school year.

5. Restrict activities if grades aren't maintained. Give more margin if and when your agreement with him is upheld.

6. Remember, the goal is to teach your teen to be a good steward of his "job" as student.

2. Homework

At the end of his sophomore year, we realized that 16-year-old Andrew's approach toward doing his homework and otherwise organizing his time was not working. Because we had addressed this issue at the beginning of his freshman year, we erroneously thought it was "handled." We got "hoodwinked" into believing that he had things under control, even though we wondered out loud how he managed to have so much time to watch TV and seemed to spend so little time doing homework. "I know what I have to do, Mom. I've got it under control. Don't worry about it."

"Don't worry about it." If I heard that phrase once, I heard it a thousand times. And unfortunately, I accepted it. Accepted it when I knew better. Accepted it when all evidence pointed to the irrefutable fact that doing schoolwork was simply not a priority for Andrew. Oh, it was in the mix, of course — on the list — but only after sports, after friends and after TV. Definitely an afterthought, not a forethought.

I think we got spoiled with 19-year-old Michael who, because of his learning disabilities, compensated for them by working twice as hard, making sure he did everything and did it well.

Of course, before Michael arrived at that point, Tom and I worked with him for years on a nightly basis, helping him with homework and teaching him various study skills to help him on his way.

Because Michael required so much and Andrew had such "natural" ability, I think we shortshrifted him — assumed he had more ability than he had because, compared to Michael, he didn't seem to require help. I think we missed the boat. I think he "looked" better than he actually was. And it was showing up "big time" at age 16.

What to do now? Well, the first thing we figured out was not to leave it up to him. We tried that during his sophomore year and, while Andrew was able to squeek his way into a "B" average, which is actually quite good, watching him do it was painful. He backed everything up to the last minute and did everything half-way, if that. Stayed up too late, got too frantic, too disorganized. Not a good way to go through school and, ultimately, not a good way to go through life.

So, we decided intervention was necessary. Necessary because what Andrew was doing was not working for him or for us. How to intervene? We knew a few things about that: 1. Yelling wasn't working. Yelling at him just got him yelling back at us, which made him not want to do anything we wanted him to do; 2. Nagging wasn't working. Nagging made him tune us out and just stay away from us; and 3. Threatening made him cajole us with promises made and promises broken, leading us to express regular disappointment in him.

We decided we needed to take a more collaborative approach because nothing we were doing was working and nothing felt good to any of us. All it did was succeed in alienating us from each other. It was enough to tell us we needed to try a different "tool."

So, we sat Andrew down one night and started by apologizing to him. We told him we were sorry — that we felt that we had shortchanged him when he was younger. Because Michael needed so much help and Andrew seemed to do so well on his own, we didn't provide some of the structure that he needed and certainly deserved to get. We also apologized for yelling and nagging at him — that from his point of view, he probably felt very shamed by us and we knew he wanted to do well but was struggling with figuring out how to get there. And so were we — struggling with how to find an effective way to help him achieve what we know he wanted to achieve.

We told him we wanted to act more like allies with him — to help him figure out how to structure his time better, to accomplish tasks better, and to feel better about himself as well.

He seemed relieved — and pleased. He readily agreed that he needed help and wanted it. He didn't like our yelling or nagging and said it made him want to avoid both us and homework. So, we started our new regimen.

We sat down with Andrew after the first few days of class and helped him think through how to organize. He wrote deadlines on a calendar. He wrote a daily plan for time management for each of his subjects. We told him he could ask us when he wanted help with a particular subject. He did — asked for help with history and ethics. I helped with history; Tom helped with ethics.

It feels so much better — to all of us. Andrew is getting things done in a more timely fashion. We're not yelling at or nagging him and we're all much more connected than we were before — we feel much more like a team — much more like a family!

TOOLS USED

1. Apologize if you feel you have done something wrong to your teen. It makes a big difference to him to hear "I'm sorry" from you. It's also good role modeling.

2. Realize that yelling and nagging rarely works and is mostly used when you feel helpless or frustrated because nothing else you've done is working

3. Set up agreed upon "homework rules," i.e. no TV, computer, phone, etc. until homework is finished. Stick to the agreement.

4. Ask about grades, classes, tests, etc. regularly and ask to see the work, tests, papers, etc. regularly.

5. Have your teen rate his own progress/performance and have him suggest a plan for improvement, if one is needed. If his plan doesn't work, implement yours.

6. If there continues to be a problem, sit and talk with your teen. Ask him what would help him succeed in this situation. Try to incorporate his wants into yours. Find a "middle" ground where you can both connect.

7. If you need one, devise a written plan that all of you can agree on and refer to when you get stuck or need clarification.

3. Extracurricular Activities

Like many households, ours is one that responds, reacts, and mostly revolves around extracurricular activities. I must confess to being one of those moms where dinner is often on the run or in between sporting events. Since both sons are heavily involved in basketball — all year round it seems — we are frequently faced with splitting off, whereby one parent takes or goes to one child's game or practice and the other parent attends or takes the second child. While I hardly see this as ideal, it is especially gratifying to watch your children doing something they totally enjoy, regardless of how skilled they are. Also, being that busy does keep them wonderfully occupied and less able to go looking for trouble or have trouble come looking for them. Our theory is "A busy child is a pretty happy child."

We find that having the structure of a sport also helps with academics — both boys do better academically when they are busiest with basketball. They use their time better and tend to focus more efficiently.

What I don't like is the frequent disruption of family mealtime. Meals done "on the road" or at a sporting event, besides being as nutritionless as possible, are simply not conducive to checking in with each other or talking about anything significant. They're more like stopping at a self-serve gas station for a quick fill-up and it doesn't matter which one you go to — they're all the same.

I miss the camaraderie of eating together in one spot. We try to compensate for some of this by insisting at other times that everyone plan on being home on a particular night so that we can spend a little time catching up with each other. If we don't make an effort at it, I tend to feel too fragmented and not enough like a family! Breaking bread together feels very essential to family life.

On the plus side, I love the ritual of going to sporting games, talking with other parents, watching the kids play and hearing all about how bad the refs were all the way home — unless of course, their team won, in which case, the refs were great. Winning is always attributed to their personal athletic skill and losing attributed to the terrible refereeing.

Regardless of outcome, however, I love that my children are involved in sports but I lament the loss of the daily family meal.

TOOLS USED

1. Extracurricular activities should be encouraged as long as grades don't suffer.

2. If family meals suffer as a result of extracurriculars, make up for some of that by making sure you schedule other family time or weekend family dinners.

3. Do not underestimate the importance of making time for family on a regular basis, with emphasis on the word "regular," even if regular only happens once or twice a week.

4. To Intervene or Not to Intervene ?

I am an admitted basketball mom so if you are not, you might want to skip this part, or just read it to see if there's something of interest or perhaps a few laughs. Ultimately chalk this section up to reflections from an "over-involved" parent!

It was the most disappointing basketball season I had had as a parent since my kids started basketball in the 4th grade. My 15-year-old, Andrew, a sophomore in high school, played on his sophomore team. He loved basketball — at least he did until the "changes" started. What changes? Changes like moving three freshmen players up to sophomore level to make the team "even better." Issues regarding fairness, playing time or the political realities of whose kid gets picked because of who his parents are.

Why should I, the parent, care about this? Why? Because it's a reflection of a larger societal problem of always looking for the best — no matter what the cost. And I was so busy looking at the cost that I was unable to see the "best" — there was too much other "stuff" in the way.

What "stuff," you might ask? For one, the fracturing of belonging. Think about it — what's the biggest need of teenagers? Isn't it, in fact, a need for belonging? To fit in? What happens to that when you have kids moving up and down in between teams? What happens when you don't have a closed door on a team? What happens to that sense of unity? Of family? I'll tell you what happens. Confusion happens. Resentment happens. Chaos happens. And poor morale happens.

Oh, I know the argument about players who should be happy just to make the team even if they never play. They know coming on the team that by the time they get into high school, they have to deal with the fact that only the "best" will be playing — no more "equal play time" for each team member. I do understand that. But something is wrong when focusing on the "best" misses some basic principles. Like what, you ask?

Like it's high school, for one. How many of these players will
be playing in college or are headed for the NBA? Not many. So
isn't the point here to build a sense of community on the team —
to build character, instill discipline, and have fun? Certainly playing well is not anathema to any of those goals and actually, the
irony here is that if you do those things, you DO build the best
team. If the players feel a sense of commitment to one another —
if they feel like a family — if they're having fun — doesn't that, in
fact, bring out their best?

How many times have we witnessed teams who come out of
nowhere to win precisely because they have all of those elements?
They don't necessarily have the greatest players but the players
they do have play with heart — and isn't it heart that helps you
win? Isn't it heart that helps you overcome shortcomings? Isn't it
heart that makes you play your best?

I think what increasingly was missing on my son's team was
heart. It was replaced by frustration, confusion and negativity,
interspersed with spots of fun and team unity. So, as a parent,
what do I do? Sit by and watch it happen because it's my son's
team, he's a sophomore and needs to deal with it himself? How
about, "This is life and he needs to learn to live with other
peoples' choices and decisions even if he doesn't agree with
them?" Or, "It's character building," "Life isn't fair," "Just deal
with it" or my favorite, "That's the way athletics is — get used
to it or get out!"

O.K. I did all of the above for awhile and all it did was make
me mad. My husband, too. I figured if he, as a man who had been
part of the athletic culture himself, was frustrated about it, then it
must be worth looking at. Plus, we send our kids to a Jesuit school
precisely because the Jesuit philosophy embodies the belief that
each child in a Jesuit institution will be enveloped in an environment that fosters the development of the whole person, not just
the "best at any cost" mentality. And don't get me wrong here.
I'm not saying I'm against going after the "best" — I'm not. What

I take issue with is the route you take to get there. I was in great disagreement with the route because I was watching the negative impact on my son.

So, what to do? Since it was my son who was directly involved, it made most sense to empower him to see what he could do to help himself. He was one of the players who got "replaced" by the freshmen moving up, so his playing time was dramatically reduced. My husband and I suggested that Andrew first write down his frustrations as well as his suggestions for change. He did that, then practiced what he would say. He kept putting off doing it — would say he was doing it "tomorrow" and when tomorrow came, there was always a reason for not doing it. So we kept reminding him it was normal to be frightened but if he wanted anything to be different, he had to let the coach know how he felt and what he thought needed to change.

To his credit, Andrew did just that and to the coach's credit, Andrew did begin to get more playing time. But even though some things got better for Andrew, the larger Jesuit "basketball philosophy" issue was still a prominent one for us. And for other parents as well, as it turned out. Other parents were frustrated not only because their kids were frustrated but because they, too, did not like where the whole basketball program was headed. Instead of focusing on the current season, all indicators were that the coaches were now concentrating solely on figuring out which players would be playing on next year's varsity — that next year's team would have so much talent on it, they would be contenders to go down state. They seemed to have forgotten all about this year's team — this year's players who had given their blood, sweat and time to a season and to coaches who were not really interested in staying in this season but who were focused on players who would enhance next year's team.

Hence, the up and down movement of players. No more "benched" varsity players playing junior varsity games — only freshmen and sophomores moving back and forth between sopho-more and varsity teams to determine who the "best" would be — for next year.

What happens to the morale of each of these teams here and now — this season? It was pretty clear that no one felt particu-larly pleased by it — not the players being replaced, not the kids moving up and down, not the parents — maybe nobody but the coaches and I even wonder how pleased they were!

So, it begs the questions, "Who is the game for anyway? The kids or the coaches? Are the kids here for the coaches or are the coaches here for the kids? Ultimately, I think both are true, but it was looking to me like some of what was important was getting lost. And, I kept thinking that I'm sending my kids to a Jesuit school, in part, so things like this don't happen. So, again, what to do?

Andrew had already spoken to his coaches — twice, in fact, so it felt like it was now our turn as parents. My husband Tom spoke to the Athletic Director about our concerns and I, along with another Mom, spoke to Andrew's two coaches. We explained our concerns about the lack of Jesuit philosophy showing itself in the program — about the frustration level of our children as well as their constant comments about not having any fun — about the whole notion of what a "man" should be. We spoke to them about our disappointment in them as coaches. To their credit, they were able to hear us — disagreed with some of what we said, but at least were respectful and listened.

So, did anything change? Not yet, although some wheels seemed to get in motion and, since the end of the season is al-most here, not much can realistically change at this point. But, as parents, we felt that we had done what we could to make our feelings known. Our son had done what he could to take care of himself. And we had spoken not only to the coaches themselves, but also to the Athletic Director, who was extremely receptive to our concerns. So much so that he let us know how much of a struggle all of this was for him — how much he hated hearing how difficult a season it had been for the kids, how it saddened him to hear how unhappy the players were and how much he wanted to be able to influence some change in the entire basketball program and was working on that. He was working to make it reflect, more obviously, the school's mission, which is to follow a Jesuit philosophy of feeding the whole person in a just and fair manner. We couldn't have asked for a better response.

Should we have intervened or interfered in the first place or should we have accepted that what was happening on these teams is simply the way things were and should be left up to the discretion of the coaches and the Athletic Director? I suppose the answer to that could be debated on both sides very convincingly. However, my belief is that with adults, just like with teenagers, you have to pick your battles and, if you feel it's an important enough issue or value to defend, then you go for it!

TOOLS USED

1. Be clear about what you expect from your teen's school, whether it be in the classroom or on the basketball court. If you choose a school based on a particular philosophy, and the school does not appear to be adhering to it, decide whether you are willing to challenge it. Also, be clear as to whether or not what you are looking for is a reasonable request based on that philosophy. In other words, don't just challenge because you think your kid deserves something that is really unrealistic or totally out of whack with what is reasonable.

2. In regard to athletics, watch what is happening on your teen's team. Determine whether school philosophy is being carried out on the court or not.

3. Write down specific behaviors or instances that reflect a consistent departure from school philosophy.

4. Be aware that what you might be challenging is an ath-letic system that is very patriarchal in its framework and not necessarily responsive to any input from you. Often any parental input is seen an "interference" or "lunatic" or "sour grapes" when, in fact, it is actually challenging an archaic system, i.e., Bobby Knight, for instance.

5. Help your teen stand up for himself if he feels he has been treated unfairly. Have him write down his concerns and practice role-playing it with you a few times before talking to his coach. Remember, you ultimately want HIM to learn how to take care of himself in these situations rather than doing it for him. Parental intervention comes in AFTER the teen tries it himself.

6. If you feel your teen is not being heard, decide whether you need to speak up yourself or let it go. You have to determine if what you are looking for is reasonable or if you are acting like an over-invested parent who is simply disappointed because your son isn't getting enough play-ing time according to YOUR assessment of his abilities. In other words, be able to separate whether your concern is real or based on the disappointment YOU feel because your teen is not playing. If you are more upset than your teen, this issue might have more to do with you and not with your son.

7. Assess whether speaking up to a coach would result in your teen being penalized. This is always a risk you take when you challenge any authority.

8. Be aware of the reality of school politics and know that a certain amount of unfairness is going to be "in the mix." It may be a matter of HOW MUCH unfairness is at work, not if there is any at all. We all know there is a certain reality about that.

9. In today's athletic culture, be mindful that there are often only two camps of thought: 1) the coach is the final and only authority; and 2) parental concern is often the result of over-involved parents. I would suggest that there is, in fact, a middle ground where our role as adults is to sometimes challenge coaches to line up behind the school's beliefs and to be authentic to the philosophy that they (the coaches) are in the school to support. Because athletics is such an important aspect of parenting, it is important to be clear about what your values are around it and to remember to separate your issues from those related to your teen.

CHAPTER
12

Friendships

1. Relationships

In our household, there has not been much dating or exclusive relationships with girls. Mostly, we have variations on the theme of "the group." The group consists of teenage boys and girls in various combinations and numbers. Sometimes "the group" numbers four or five, sometimes it's 15, 20 or 25. I feel like I constantly ask the question, "who are you going to be with?" and get a variety of possibilities and mixtures.

There does seem to be a "core" of three to five kids in "the group" and some kids don't get along with some of the other kids, so there is some concern about "mixing" two groups together — sort of like oil and water. Mostly, though, they travel in a pack. And they move from house to house.

One big issue that seems to come up fairly regularly happens when a boy and girl within the group become attracted to one another. Inevitably they ponder whether dating will "ruin" their friendship. In 17-year-old Michael's case, he seems to land on the side of not dating, preferring to keep the girls as friends. In his words "having a girlfriend is too much work. They like to talk on the phone a lot and get their feelings hurt too easily. I'm too busy and they take up too much time — maybe later. I prefer to keep them as friends."

Andrew, at 14, has a core of two-three friends and different groups of girls come in and out of that core. He also seems to see girls as "high maintenance," doesn't like long phone conversations with them, but really does enjoy the group gatherings, walking from house to house in the neighborhood.

I can say I'm surprised neither of them has been interested in a one-on-one relationship, but also relieved. I think they have plenty of time for that. I like that they get to know girls as friends and my hope is that they will translate and carry that over and into dating relationships. For now, though, I find comfort in them being part of "the pack."

TOOLS USED

1. Encourage your teen to hang out in boy/girl groups. It helps him learn how to make and build friendships.

2. Don't let the groups get too large. If they do, the "group stupidity" quotient tends to rise.

3. Applaud him for not branching off into one-on-one relationships too early.

4. Use his friendships with the opposite sex as an opportunity to teach him that healthy, long-term relationships are built on friendships first. Teach him the differences between a healthy and an unhealthy relationship. Of course, it helps if you are in a healthy relationship yourself, since you are his first role model.

2. Preparing to Prepare to Go Out

"I don't know. I haven't gotten that far yet."

These are the familiar words I hear as I ask 16-year-old Andrew what his plans are for this Friday night. And it's already 4:30 p.m. on Friday! I should know better. I should know that this response is what I get almost every time I ask him, on a weekend, what his plans are. Silly me, thinking that my son would actually plan social time in advance. What planet was I on?

I was on the parent planet, of course. The one that wishes my kids would make a social plan and actually stick to it. Actually have an answer like "Yeah, Mom, we're going over to so and so's house for the night and I'll be home by curfew." Fat chance — no chance, really. The only time teenagers' plans seem to be set in stone is when there is an athletic activity and even then, they are unclear what they are doing either before or after that event.

And what I have further discovered after years of observing this behavior is that that is precisely the point. That the end result — "the plan" — is precisely what interests them the least. They are all about preparing to prepare to plan, not actually carrying OUT the plan. They are on the phone non-stop, one calling the other, the other calling yet another — the "usual" hang around group as well as the "not so usual" hang around group. Various combinations of plans. Who's picking up whom, whose house to start at, who's driving, who can go, who can't — all of it part of that start-up drama for the evening. And I am increasingly convinced that that part of it — the preparation — is by far the most exciting part of the evening for them.

How do I know that, you ask? I know that because I have observed, time after time, that once they arrive at their "destination," whether it's someone's home or the McDonald's or the outside basketball court, or "just walking around," that they then get busy planning again.

"What's next?" Cell phones start up. There's the check-in with other kids to see what "they're" doing — checking to see if they might possibly be missing something more interesting or exciting — something going on somewhere else. Can't miss an opportunity if one happens to be floating around!

Furthermore, don't ever count on whatever "plan" they start out with, either. For instance, last night Andrew planned to go to his friend Stewart's, followed by a basketball game at the local school gym, followed by a return to our house. It then actually started at Peter's house, followed by a visit to Jane's and then everyone back home. So, I'm thinking he's on plan #1, which is what he TOLD me, but he actually ends up DOING plan #32, which I don't often find out about until after he gets home. And the latter example is definitely more of the norm.

I must admit that this pattern used to make me nuts — nuts, because my expectation was that when you make a plan, you basically stick to the plan. What is so difficult about that? I have

since learned that making a plan and sticking to it is terribly boring and constraining for teenagers and is to be avoided as often as
possible. My solution? Stop being frustrated — laugh about it —
equip them with a cell phone and plan not to be surprised when
what you THOUGHT they were going to do in no way resembles
the end result!

TOOLS USED

1. Don't be surprised when "plans" change frequently —
   even by the minute.

2. Expect the unexpected.

3. Still, ask him for "the Plan," but expect it to change.

4. Have him let you know as he moves from one locale to
   another. Expect that to happen regularly.

5. Use humor around this issue.

6. Don't assume he is being "cagey" with you or lying when
   he changes plans so frequently — he really isn't. He is
   simply invested in the process, not the end result.

7. Equip him with a cell phone so you can track him as
   needed. Remember, the cell phone is for YOUR conve-
   nience, not his!

3. The Cost of Roaming

Andrew had just started roaming around the neighborhood with four of his friends when it happened. He was surprised and angry — I was saddened but knew it was a matter of when it would happen, not if. What was the "It?" It was his first experience being stopped and frisked by the police.

Here they were, four 14-year-old teenagers walking around the neighborhood carrying a bucket filled with water balloons. In their minds, they were looking for an "interesting" place to have a water balloon fight. It was too boring doing it at our house. They had gotten "antsy" with Play Station and decided they wanted to "see what was going on" elsewhere. So they filled up their balloons and went out roaming.

As it happened, on that particular night, one of the neighborhood girls had been assaulted and hit with a stick by another group of teenagers. The police were out looking for that group when they spotted Andrew, his friends and the bucket. It didn't help that Andrew and group had just emerged loud and laughing from an alley, making them look pretty interesting to the police. So the boys were told to spread eagle against the squad car and were in the process of being frisked when a friend of ours husband (who was driving by looking for the group with the stick) recognized Andrew and the others and stopped to inquire. That was really lucky for the boys. He vouched that these boys were not part of the group the police were looking for, piled the boys into his car and they all went looking for the other group. Never did find them.

Apparently that was enough excitement for one night and the boys were delivered home.

What I found interesting in all of this is the fact that Andrew waited a while before telling the "police frisking me" portion of the story. He told everything else, but waited until the end. when he finally said, "Oh, by the way, we got stopped by the police."

I, of course, wanted every sordid detail and as he told the story, he got madder and madder. He talked about how unfair and discriminating it was — said if it were a group of old people walking down the street, the police would barely have looked at them, much less stopped and frisked them.

I agreed, and then went on to talk about the difference between what is fair and what is life. No, it wasn't fair that they got stopped since they hadn't been doing anything wrong, but the reality is, they were four teenage boys coming out of an alley carrying a bucket, laughing and talking loud. To some people, that looks threatening — and their appearance did occur in the neighborhood where a crime was recently committed by a group of teenagers. So having the police stop them made sense — at least to the police.

This was Andrew's first foray into being treated unfairly as a teenager, just because of how he looked, his age and the fact that he was in a group. He didn't like it and I didn't like it either but, he must understand that this experience is part of what awaits him as he goes about the business of being a teenager in this neighborhood and in this world today. He has become part of a group that is often seen as "trouble," and he needs to figure out his choices as he navigates his way through these years. And we all have to find a way to live with that because it's not about fair or unfair — it's simply the way it is.

TOOLS USED

1. As your teen starts going out with friends into various neighborhoods, plan on your anxiety level rising — for a few years.

2. Tell your teen — and his friends — to steer away from confrontations and not to get "macho."

3. Share stories about teens who made good decisions and those who made bad ones — and the ingredients that go into each.

4. Talk about the "group mentality" — how groups of teenagers can easily escalate into doing stupid things — and how to catch themselves before that happens.

5. Give him a plan of action. For example: If in trouble, first try to get away, then call police, or call home.

6. Equip your teen with a cell phone — not for *his* comfort, but for yours.

4. Teen-Only Vacations — Yes or No?

We thought we had been quite clear with our 17-year-old senior. And actually, as I think back on it, we had. Michael had "informed" or "warned" us in the fall of his senior year that he would be going on spring vacation with his friends and we shouldn't count on him for our usual family spring break vacation.

The argument was predictable: it was his last vacation before finishing high school, all of his friends would be attending different colleges; every one of his friends' parents were allowing their sons to go away without supervision; he is a responsible person who exercises good judgment and won't do anything stupid — he's the one who keeps other kids from acting stupid.

Blah, blah, blah, I thought at the time. No amount of schmoozing or convincing or cajoling would get me to move off of my solid pedestal of belief that teenagers could not be trusted in a group in a warm climate on vacation without an adult present. I still shudder when I think of the images that picture conjures up: drunken teenagers on the beach or, worse yet, in a hotel room drinking and either trying or successfully having sex.

So, it didn't matter what Michael would say — I wasn't budging. No vacation with friends unless a parent was present. Period.

Persistent child that he is, Michael checked into hotel prices, airfares, etc., in warm climates and asked his friends' parents if anyone would be willing to chaperone. Notice he did not want his own parents to be the chaperones — only other teens' parents. As it happened, two parents expressed some hesitant willingness to chaperone the group of eight teens — until one of the teens asked if it would be OK if he drank provided his parents gave written permission.

That was enough to stop the Moms from taking on that group responsibility. Secretly I was relieved because it meant Michael wouldn't be going anywhere with friends. So, I happily planned our usual family vacation — six days in Orlando, just the four of us. It sounded good to me. In passing one day, I mentioned to Michael that we had made our Easter travel plans and was delighted he would be joining us. He promptly informed me he'd rather stay home with his extremely protective grandmother for a week than go on a boring family vacation. He further promised that, if he was forced to go, he would make it the most miserable trip we ever had. So much for my thinking he had let go of the idea of a "teen-only" vacation and had reluctantly but quietly resolved himself to going with us on a lovely family vacation.

Not so. Up it started again — the protests, the pleading, the promises, the reasonings — the hardest part was listening to him use all of the communication skills we had taught him over the years. He was now using them on us and doing quite a good job of it — both Tom and I were being influenced to change our positions. I wanted to throttle Michael for actually making sense and trying to reason with us. Frankly, it was easier to say no to him when he was acting like a sulky teenager who wouldn't take no for an answer.

When he started acting like a rational adult and presented a "case" for being a responsible teenager who was looking forward to having fun with his friends and not an alcoholic teen who couldn't wait to get away from home and parents so he could drink and party, it really made me stop and listen. Either he was actually making sense or I was getting completely snowed and would be truly sorry later. Who am I kidding? I was already sorry — I knew I was getting swayed when I stopped wanting to say "Yes, but" after every sentence he made and instead started saying things like "Good point" or "Yes you're right." I couldn't believe my own ears!

We ultimately agreed to let him go as long as he agreed to a plan. The agreed-upon plan was that Michael and seven friends would stay in two condos in a family resort in Naples. He would be in touch with us on his cell phone every day. In addition, a meeting with all of the teens plus their parents would be planned beforehand so the ground rules would be made and agreed upon by everyone. Michael agreed to everything. He also reminded us that he was going away to college in four months — that we had given him good tools over the years — so when were we going to trust him to start using them on his own?

He was right and try as I would to poke holes in his reasoning, the bottom line for me was whether I was going to let my worry and fear make my decision or my trust in my son. I voted for trusting my son, and I do feel that that was a good decision.

Michael was feeling quite proud of himself for how "adultly" he handled this situation and confident he would live up to his promises. I was mostly confident that he would, although I had anxiety all around my edges and found myself engaging in superstitions like crossing my fingers and promising God that I would do whatever he wanted as long as this vacation ended with no calamities. Other than that, I think the event left me completely ambivalent — happy to know my son wanted to and was prepared to use the toolbox we gave him and at the same time scared to let him go so he could use it.

I still felt compelled to be there, though, to tell him exactly what tools to use and when to use them.

The end result of all my worry was that Michael had a wonderful time on his vacation and came back very much alive. The biggest complaint lodged against "the group" was about noise at 4 a.m. — quite reasonable I would say. I wouldn't want to vacation next to a group of 18-year-olds either — would you?

TOOLS USED

1. Don't encourage teen-only vacations. Decide whether your teen is mature enough to handle one.

2. If he keeps nagging until you can't take it anymore, and you are willing to consider it, make sure your teen has a

specific plan. Cover plane tickets, hotel room, limited number of teens, agreement about drinking behaviors.

3. Have a parent/teen meeting prior to the trip. Emphasize expectations about his behavior.

4. Have your teen check-in daily during the trip.

5. Cross your fingers — wish them a good time — try not to worry.

6. Set up negative consequences should your teen decide to break the rules.

7. Restrict destinations. In Mexico, for example, the legal drinking age is 18, so this may not be one of your choices, although it will probably be one of his!

CHAPTER 13

Spirituality in The Family

1. Religion/Spirituality

Ambivalence is what seems to best describe our family expression and experience of religion and spirituality. Having been raised Catholic, received Catholic education up through college, left the Church and returned years later, deciding to raise our children Catholic was a good, but ambivalent decision. We wanted to make sure they were raised with some religious base, one that they could either embrace or leave, as they got older. And Catholicism is what we knew and felt most comfortable with. So, return we did. And sent our children to Catholic schools as well.

Dotted in-between the Catholic experience were periodic forays to Unity Church, since their philosophy was closer to our own spiritual beliefs than the Catholic Church. However, the Unity Church we attended did not have much regarding instruction for children, so we were ambivalent about fully embracing that church too. Consequently, we satisfied our ambivalent spiritual appetite by attending one, the other, or both churches at various times while raising the kids.

In addition to that, or instead of either of these churches, we would sometimes sit around the kitchen table, light a candle, sing a song, read a meditation from one of our favorite books, then talk about what it meant to each of us. The boys really liked this option because it didn't require driving anywhere and usually took only about 20 minutes, at most. They would sometimes beg for this option — not , of course, because they loved it, but because it was relatively painless and best of all, quick.

To this day we are ambivalent. We require the boys to attend church with us when either of us has to lector, which ends up being about once a month. They both attend Catholic services at their respective schools, so we do know they have a faith base that is part of the core of their being. However, active involvement in our local church has been sporadic for us as a family. We have struggled with the fact that the Catholic church has so many of its own problems and dysfunctions. Because of that, how can we justify going there, hoping to be inspired? And how can we inspire our sons if we feel ambivalent ourselves?

Most of the time we come away from church annoyed because the sermon was irrelevant, the priest was not understandable, or it was just plain boring. However, we do want to be part of a community of faith, so we do participate to a certain degree. And we talk about that with the boys. They understand our ambivalence, our wish for them to have a foundational faith base, and they accept the fact that we are what is commonly referred to as "cafeteria Catholics." That's OK with us. We do invite our kids to join us at church or at church-sponsored events and they do when in town or when they feel like coming. We do not force them. Part of why we don't is because we do have a strong sense of spirituality within our home, so we find a lot of comfort in that. We encourage our teenagers to think about a higher power and to think about how that power works in their lives. When we discuss issues with them, God is a part of the fiber of these discussions. It is normal for them to think in terms of what purpose God has for them in this life and to figure out what gifts they have to bring to the world. Going to church is an optional part of their faith life, but having God as an important part of how they think and how they make decisions is not an option. It's part of the "weave" of their lives, both at home and at school. We do encourage and remind them in various ways to make room for a God presence in their daily lives, and to use God as a vehicle for making any major decisions in their lives.

TOOLS USED

1. Be as clear as possible in letting your teens know where you stand on the subject of religion and/or spirituality.

2. Talk with them about how you arrived at your belief system.

3. Encourage them to join you in your practice of spirituality or to pick something else that feels like a better fit for them.

4. If they choose something different, don't alienate yourself from them — join them in their services or express an interest in learning more about what they believe or practice.

5. Talk about religion/spirituality as a regular and normal part of family conversations.

2. Is That God Talking?

It was fall of sophomore year. As I was putting a load of laundry in, Michael came home from school, threw his book bag down on the floor and proceeded to go into a litany of how upset he was because he didn't know how to say "No." I had no clue what he was talking about, so I said, "What's the matter?" He then began blurting out how one of the neighborhood girls had asked him to the Homecoming dance at her school and how he was caught off guard and ended up saying "Yes" when he didn't want to go at all. He was mad at himself for saying yes.

It had nothing to do with her, he assured me. She's nice and pretty — but. Then he launches into a litany of all the things he expects will happen. "I won't know anyone else ... I don't know how to dance ... If we go with guys from another school, they'll hate me ... I'll miss being with my friends."

On and on he raged about all the imagined horrible things that would happen to him if he went.

I initially made the mistake of challenging him — to suggest that maybe those things wouldn't happen — just maybe he'd actually have a great time. Well, that was a big mistake. He clearly did not want to hear that — he was too invested in the "horror" of it and couldn't see anything else. And he was getting mad at me for suggesting that there could possibly be another way to look at this situation. He was definitely seeing only one color — and it was bleak.

So, in a moment of wisdom, I decided to just shut up and listen and stop challenging him. Definitely a better choice. I would periodically say something like "Anything else you want to say about it?" or "Yeah, you look pretty mad about it" or I'd just nod my head as he talked — or ranted. A much better choice.

He probably went on for about 10 or 15 minutes about this horrible decision he had made and how was he going to get out of it. Now, I had a bit of an investment in the decision he would ultimately make because the girl who had asked him was the daughter of a friend of mine. So, I was having a hard time not telling him what I thought the right thing to do was. But, having learned a little from my first mistake in this conversation, I decided not to throw that in and to try a different approach.

I told him that he was the one who had to make this decision, but I would ask that he consider two things before he decided: 1) Don't make a decision while you're angry. Go punch the punching bag or work out or run until you feel like you got all the "mad" out; and 2) Pray about it. Pray for some guidance and then pay attention — that an answer will show up.

He rolled his eyes but did agree to that so I went away for a while and left him alone. I came back an hour later and asked him how he was doing. He said he did the punching bag thing and did feel better — also prayed — but he hadn't noticed any answer. Then he admitted that the biggest reason he didn't think he could go to the dance was because he had lost his school ID and he couldn't get into any dance without it. That reason seemed to clinch his resolve that this was out of his hands and a very legitimate reason for not going.

I said to pray some more and pay attention to any messages or thoughts that came up. Then I went away again. I came back another hour later and asked again how he was doing. He said that while doing his religion homework one of the readings was about "doing the right thing."

"Was that God talking?" he asked. I replied, "You have to decide that."

He continued, "I still don't think I can go because I don't have a student ID and I can't get one until Monday — and that's after the dance. Is that God talking?" I didn't have time to answer because at that very moment the phone rang. I didn't recognize the woman's voice, but what she said made me laugh out loud. She gave her name and said she had found Michael's wallet out in the snow — his wallet that had his student ID in it! She was going to send it back in the mail, she said, but she got a "funny feeling" about it today and decided to call instead!

Michael had been listening intently and his eyes kept getting wider and wider as he heard my end of the conversation. I agreed to pick up the wallet right then, especially since she only lived a few blocks away from us.

When I got off the phone, Michael and I both looked at each other and said, "That was God talking." He and I went to pick up the wallet and the woman reiterated once again how she had the wallet in an envelope to send the next day, but got a "funny feeling" about it that afternoon and decided to call the phone number in the wallet.

Was that God talking? Don't know. Just know that Michael saw it that way and made the decision to go to the dance without any input from me and he had a good time. He did learn an important lesson about the use of prayer in his life as well as not making assumptions about situations and that these lessons feel like very important tools to have in the toolbox of life.

TOOLS USED

1. Ask your teen what's wrong if you notice he's upset.

2. Be prepared to listen — without interruption or trying to problem-solve.

3. Ask the question: "Did you want to say anything more about that?" after he has told you basic information.

4. Make reflective listening comments, such as "You sound really upset about that" or "I see you're really mad about that" rather than trying to problem-solve for him. Remember, being empathic with your teen doesn't mean you are agreeing with him.

5. Ask him if he would like your help solving the problem.

6. Acknowledge his suggestions and add some of your own, but, if appropriate, don't tell him what to do.

7. Suggest he take some time away from the situation and come back to it later.

8. Discuss the spiritual ramifications of the situation with him. Invite him to think about what happened from a spiritual perspective.

3. A Crescendo Moment

One of the most powerful experiences I have had as a parent was the result of observing my 17-year-old son at the end of a Jesuit Kairos retreat that he had attended. For three days he was away at a retreat center with 34 fellow male students as well as a few faculty and student leaders. The focus was on seeing and developing their relationship with God. Exercises and reflections were designed so the students could get real with each other, share with each other and see the "Godliness" in each of them, highlight the similarities rather than the differences and understand how to carry that forward.

The true highlight of the retreat was the reading of parental letters — out loud — to each student in front of the entire group. Each parent was to write a love letter to their sons — only positive remarks. These letters were a surprise to each student — the boys had no idea they were coming. Not only was each parent invited to write a letter, but siblings, relatives and friends were also invited to write about how they appreciated and loved the person they were writing to. Michael received about 40 letters — some from his close friends, some from former teachers and students, some from students he barely knew and some that he didn't know at all but who knew him. He said he was blown away to read and hear how much he was valued and loved by those in his life — he had no idea how much he mattered to the people around him.

On the last day of the retreat, parents and former Kairos participants were invited to the closing ceremony. The boys had no idea any of us would be there. It was wonderful to watch their faces light up as they walked into a room full of people who cared about them and came to celebrate the richness of this experience.

We were treated to testimony after testimony from each of these boys about what a transforming experience this retreat had been for them. It was refreshing and profound to watch as they

shared their feelings, hugged each other, and claimed their close-
ness and bond in front of fellow classmates and family members.
To see such "openness, honesty, and love" — particularly between
and among boys — was satisfying, joyful and hopeful at the same
time. To see them fill up on the love that was in the room made
me so grateful and proud. And those feelings grew even stronger
through the next day.

Michael asked his Dad and me to go out to lunch the next
day so he could share his retreat experience in more detail. We, of
course, were delighted — even more so because Michael initiated
the invitation. It was so touching to hear him relate so easily and
excitedly all the lessons he learned during this special time. His
most profound lesson, he said, was learning not to make fun of
people anymore. He had heard story after story about the hurt
and pain caused by being made fun of. He never realized how
hurtful that could be. He also elaborated on his profound gratitude for his own life — his family and the abundance in his life in
all areas.

Here was my son, at 17-years-old, able to share his deep feelings and gratitude with us in a way that just made my heart swell
with admiration and pride. How often do we, as parents, have
that opportunity with our children? I was getting it and was not
going to miss a minute of the specialness of this moment.

To make this an even more poignant experience — as if it
weren't already a crescendo moment — Michael invited us to read
the letters people wrote to him. Talk about mind-blowing — letter after letter from person after person highlighted Michael's sen-
sitivity, his ability to stand up for others, especially those who
were made fun of — his tremendous work ethic and his leader-
ship qualities, both on and off the basketball court.

Can't you just imagine how full I was with admiration, appreciation and love for this person — my son? This was definitely a
very rich and profound set of moments. Moments that I want to
catalogue and remember on other good days as well as on darker

days — on days when I forget or he forgets who his best self is or I've forgotten my own "best self." These kind of days reach out to me to remind me of why I am here and they really do make me want to love more and reach out more. They really do fill me up from the inside out. It is these kinds of moments that lead our children to feeling better about themselves and behaving better in the world. As schmaltzy as it sounds, this experience truly reminded me of the profound power of love. May I remember that the next time I want to reach for anger or hate and may my son remember that as well.

TOOLS USED

1. Really cherish those open, vulnerable moments with your teen.

2. Let him know how important/meaningful they are to you.

3. Remember how wonderful your teen is, particularly on days when he is not exhibiting his "best" self.

4. Realize that "showing up" for these kind of events with your teen sets the stage for good communication and good connections.

5. Share with your teen any similar experiences you may have had in your life.

4. Teenage Death

He had been in Michael's Freshman English class — Steve — nice, quiet kid; had asthma. Not a friend, but an acquaintance. After school one day, Steve and a couple of friends smoked some marijuana, then went to the local shopping mall. While at the mall, Steve began to have an asthma attack. He had forgotten his medication or couldn't find it and went into cardiac arrest. He subsequently died.

The effect on Michael was strong, even though he didn't know Steve well. It was amazing to Michael that you could literally be here one day and gone the next. It was "weird" to be in class and see his empty seat or walk past the locker that still held his things. And going to the wake was very sad. Listening to and seeing the despair of Steve's family and feeling powerless to help them was very difficult for Michael.

We talked to Michael about the precariousness of life — the fact that there are no insurance policies we can buy to guarantee a long life. Whether or not Steve smoking marijuana that particular day influenced his asthma attack and subsequent death we'll never know. But sometimes doing something minor results in something major. Some mistakes are unforgiving.

TOOLS USED

1. Talk to your teen about death. Because teenagers often feel "invincible," they tend to believe that death can't happen to people in their age group.

2. Talk about how decisions don't seem, on the face of it, to be any big deal, i.e. smoking a joint or having a drink, but they can sometimes result in very tragic endings.

3. Share any stories that you read or run across to help raise your teen's awareness regarding the impact of choices and

the consequences of those choices. Because they tend to forget rather quickly, bring it up regularly to keep it in their consciousness.

CHAPTER 14

Making Time for Family

1. Family Time

We had decided to do a fairly low-key vacation which, for us, meant staying in the Midwest and not running around everyday seeing and doing a multitude of things. So, off we went to French Lick, Indiana to a resort for one week to enjoy some much needed "family time."

Well, anyone who's been to French Lick knows that it's home to Larry Bird — the house he grew up in is on the train ride through the town. It's a very quiet area with lots of golf courses and not a lot to do. Our children were completely bored by day two. We did our best, playing board games, card playing, swimming and of course some golfing. We were having an O.K. time, but it became pretty clear that doing this for an entire week would be tortuous for us all.

So, we decided we'd leave after five days and that, on the last day, we'd have a pleasant family round of golf, just the four of us. Well, at about the 8th hole it started drizzling, but, hey, we were just going to plod on, having fun.

At the 9th hole, our 16-year-old son Michael was frustrated because he wasn't playing well, so he threw his golf club down. Andrew, our 13-year-old, was horsing around with his club and ended up swinging it, hitting Michael on his already swollen knee. Well that was clearly the end of harmonious family time. Michael started swearing at Andrew, running after him, Mom was yelling at both Andrew and Michael, and Dad was trying to calm everyone down. On top of everything, it was now raining steadily. So, with everyone mad and frustrated, we decided to stop playing and go home.

Andrew was so upset at being blamed for what he considered to be accidental that he refused to drive back to the room with us and, instead, walked the mile back to the room. This was not exactly what Tom and I had pictured as a pleasant ending to our vacation.

Tom and I decided a family meeting was in order before we would begin our drive home. Nobody was feeling good about what happened and we felt we must clear the air before we left.

Everyone was given a chance to express how they felt about what had happened, and, after some degree of yelling and mutual blaming, apologies were made all around. We then had a bit of a family hug and proceeded to laugh much of the way home about how this was one of the worst family trips we ever had. But the irony of it was, admitting that the trip was disappointing to all of us made it a bonding experience for us at the same time and it gave us permission to leave early. We still laugh about it to this day!

TOOLS USED

1. If you're having a bad time, acknowledge it. See if the vacation can be "retrieved" by switching plans or going home early.

2. If conflicts occur that aren't resolved, call a "family meeting" to discuss it.

3. Listen to everyone's point of view/perspective on the conflict. Don't take sides. Hear everyone out.

4. Ask each person how he/she would like to resolve conflicts. Use humor as "buffer" or "balm."

2. Holiday Rituals

It was like pulling teeth to get it to happen, but in the end, well worth it. We usually put up our Christmas tree on the day after Thanksgiving but, for the last two years, because of basketball tournaments, we have had to find an alternative date. This year we decided it was to be Sunday night, after both boys' basketball practice and after Tom's meeting. Tom and I had already set up the artificial tree, ahead of time, and Michael agreed to do the lights so that the four of us could spend our collective time putting on the ornaments. But before we got to that part, we had to decide on "ambiance."

The boys wanted to watch a movie while we decorated the tree. Tom and I said, "absolutely not — Christmas carols only." This statement resulted in many protestations by both boys about our "stupid oldies" music and how "boring" it would make the process for them. We held firm, however, saying they could pick the music, but we would be playing carols while we decorated. Reluctantly, Andrew picked out the least repulsive of the CD's and proceeded to put it on. In the meantime, I was unwrapping all of the ornaments and making announcements about each one I unwrapped — at least those I remembered. And this part was the most fun because at this point the boys really got into it.

One of the rituals Tom and I have is to get each of the boys an ornament every year to put on the tree. We started it when they were born, so they have at least one special ornament for each year of their lives. So, of course, as we were unwrapping and announcing, they wanted to make sure all of their respective ornaments were there and any one of us would then recall the circumstances or story around each one. Then the fun really began for them. Both boys wanted to make sure all of their own ornaments were placed front and center on the tree — none of them could be near the bottom or in the back. We laughed like hyenas when Michael or Andrew would replace the other's ornament and put it in a less desirable spot on the tree. Then we took turns taking silly pictures of each other in front of the tree or they'd make fun of me because I love to "belt out" the Christmas carols. I then reminded them that this ritual really is a lot of fun and maybe they shouldn't come kicking and screaming to it — rather, cherish and appreciate it. Michael responded that he would definitely appreciate it when he gets older and that right now it is fun, but it doesn't feel like "cherishing" material — it's just something we do as a family. Little do they know how very cherishing and special that is.

TOOLS USED

1. Make sure you develop and/or continue family rituals.

2. Treat these rituals as "sacred" — don't let your teens' whining deter you from them. They will appreciate and continue them when they get to be adults.

3. Have some "middle" ground around how you do the rituals if you get a lot of resistance from your teen.

4. Talk to your teens about the importance of rituals and how you would like them to carry these rituals on as they become adults and have their own families.

5. Take home movies if you can and look at them every year as part of the holiday ritual.

3. Mother/Son Bonding

Eighteen-year-old Michael needed to see one more play for his theater class. The problem was he had forgotten about it and now he had only four days in which to accomplish the task. "Would you help me?" he asked.

I thought of not doing it — of making him do all the looking and calling for reservations. That would teach him not to pro-crastinate — to get things done on time. The only problem with that argument was that Michael almost always gets things done early, if not on time. Coming down to the 11th hour really was unusual for him. He probably really did forget. So I decided to explore options that would work for the four-day time frame and see what happened.

The choices ended up being fairly slim since it was right after the Christmas holidays. But I did find a local production — near the house — on a Thursday night. Great combo — Michael was delighted and I was looking forward to spending some time with him experiencing some culture.

I was also recalling the fact that the last time he and I at-tended a play together was when he was 14. At that time, Tom and I had decided that the boys needed to get a regular dose of theater and so with some friends we subscribed to a large Chicago production company and required each of the boys to accom-pany us every other play. That way each of them would have some special time with their parents and would also be getting a taste of good theater. Good in theory. In practice, they rarely went — either homework or disinterest stopped them, and the one time Michael did go — also his first time, by the way — was to see Death of a Salesman. When asked after the play what he thought of it, he promptly replied, "What do you think I thought? I'm a 14-year-old whiney teenager. This is a play about a lonely man in a dysfunctional family. I think it was depressing and it sucked!" So much for the exposure to culture!

So I'm thinking this play at this point in time could be a reparative experience. The play was about the relationship between a man and a woman who worked together and had a one-night stand. I'm thinking this could be an opportunity for us to talk about relationships and how they work or don't work — what it means to slowly pursue a relationship — anything along those lines — or just some time to spend together having some fun.

We did definitely have fun, but it did not at all happen the way I thought it would. First of all, the theater was a tiny storefront with gates on the front windows directly across from the "L" station. There were only 36 seats and it was so hot, we could barely stand it. We were sitting up near the ceiling in front of two girls who turned out to be the 16- and 11-year-old daughters of the main actor (there were only two actors in the play.)

Also it was "opening night" and there were 25 people in the audience. The set was made to look like someone's studio apartment. The bed was quite prominent on the set, which should have been a red flag to me. But it wasn't. So, the play begins in darkness — then all you hear is moaning — first the man, then the woman. I'm thinking that there's either going to be an opening sex scene or something totally ludicrous, making you think that it was a sex scene, but not. I was hoping for the latter. No such luck.

The lights go on and yep, there they are, a man and a woman lying in bed — partially covered — but very naked. And for the next 45 minutes, the play explored the relationship between these two with lots of sexual innuendo and lots of sexual content and lots of sexual touch. At one point, the man says "I love your body. Can I just look at it for awhile?" And she obliges, with a 15 second look — how accommodating!

By the time intermission came, Michael looked completely mortified and said he couldn't take anymore. Could he wait in the car if I wanted to see the rest of the play? I said I was fine with leaving. I told the girls behind us their father was doing a good job and Michael and I discreetly grabbed our things and tried to look as if we were just going outside to get some air. Once out, we quickly walked away down the street and promptly started laughing. Michael's first response was "Oh my God, I can't believe I just saw a porno play sitting next to my mother! I can't wait to go to class tomorrow and report on this one! It won't matter that I didn't see the end of it!"

In between laughing bouts, I was struggling to make a case for the "aesthetic and cultural learning" from the play, but even I felt like I was stretching. I did emphasize the "exposure" aspect of going to this kind of play and we both cracked up over this as well. Michael was further mortified by the fact that the actor's daughters were watching their Dad in this kind of play and said, "I would die if you or Dad ever did anything like that. I'd never be able to go watch you. Oh my God, my mother naked on stage. I would absolutely die! Promise me you'll never do that!"

"No danger of that," I replied!

We continued to laugh all the way home. I did try to intersperse our laughing with getting Michael to see some redeeming value in having seen this play but, I must admit, I wasn't convinced myself. So, we had a great bonding experience, but nothing like I thought it was going to be. And maybe that's the best learning — that you never know how something is going to turn out, but at least you expose yourself to the experience. And if worse comes to worse, you can always laugh.

TOOLS USED

1. Always check out/research what you are going to see before you set it up with your teen.

2. If it turns out you've made a mistake, leave.

3. If it doesn't work out, laugh at it with your child. Try to find a way to take something positive from your shared experience.

4. Look for any lessons you learned from this experience and share them with your child.

5. Appreciate the time you have together, regardless of the circumstances and let him know how good it feels to spend time with him. It really matters to him to hear you say it, even if he brushes it off or makes it appear as if it's no big deal. It is.

4. Laughter

I love that we are able to laugh in our family. We laugh about a lot of things, but mostly we laugh about each other and all of our little oddities. We affectionately make fun of each other and ourselves with great frequency. Tom, my husband, often provides the boatload of material for us to poke fun at. We often recall with great hilarity the time when we were putting up Christmas decorations outside and 16-year-old Michael was asked to put lights on the bushes all around the house. Michael did, but he neglected to make sure that all the lights actually worked when he strung them up. Well, Tom was a bit short-tempered then and when he saw the lights that were out, told Michael to redo them. Michael forgot or was too tired or didn't want to, so when Tom went out later to turn on the lights and saw that they hadn't been fixed, he started yelling.

"The lights, the lights — you didn't do the lights!"

Because it was uncharacteristic of him to yell like that, Michael, Andrew and I started laughing. So, of course, Tom got even madder — for a minute. Then, once he saw us doubled over in laughter, all yelling "The lights, the lights!" he started laughing too. Once his anger had dissipated, we could then tell Michael to go out and finish the job properly. Which he did, happily I think, because we had used laughter instead of anger to achieve cooperation.

Ever since this incident, if one of us gets irrational or bent out of shape, someone will start saying "The lights! The lights!" and usually we can laugh about it — not all the time, mind you, but often enough. It's a really good tool to have in the family box.

TOOLS USED

1. If you can laugh about something rather than yell about something, choose laughter. It feels better and can be very effective at achieving the end result you want.

2. Find reasons to laugh. Remember that laughter can bridge a lot of sore spots. Use it with regularity. But also be mindful of when it is inappropriate. Know the difference.

5. Ordinary Time

Today was one of those days — a day-off day. It was Columbus Day or Founder's Day, as some call it. No matter what you call it, it's a day off for the kids. And basically, if it's an off day for the kids, it's an off day for me too.

Since the kids were little, I have tried to make their off days my off days. I work for myself, so I can basically determine my own schedule. And I like to be around when they are, even as teenagers — especially as teenagers. Because they tend to be out of the house so much, I really like to be around them during the day, even if we just end up hanging around, each doing our own thing.

This particular day, their Dad had gone to work and both boys were up early doing their homework. I ended up helping each of them with their respective writing projects and even though it can be hard helping them as opposed to doing the work for them, it's just being with them that I truly enjoy.

This particular day, Andrew was writing a school story about basketball, and we really laughed a lot as he was brainstorming the details of the story. Michael, on the other hand, was having a harder time expressing his thoughts for his paper, so working with him was a bit more challenging. Again, the trick was to "help" and not to "do for" them.

At any rate, both boys completed their projects with me moving from helping one to helping the other interspersed with doing laundry or reading or writing. I then suggested we go out to lunch. I love this part because it allows us to go out to a restaurant, share a meal and share conversation. Somehow going out to eat, maybe because we do it so rarely, invokes a different kind and level of sharing that we don't always get to do around the kitchen table.

So today we went out for Thai food and talked about body image and self-esteem of older women. I had watched Oprah that morning and that was the topic. The boys were laughing like crazy at some of the descriptions of what some older women will do to try and look younger. They, of course, thought it was ridiculous, in part because it is so irrelevant to their lives but also just because it's not something that would occur to them to think about at all.

At any rate, it ended up being pretty eye-opening to them. They had never thought about how the media invites women, and men as well, to be young, beautiful and thin. No matter how old you are, the goal is not to look it. We had such a good time talking and laughing about it. It really didn't matter what the topic was — it was simply a chance for the three of us to be together, sharing a meal and enjoying each other's company. I so remember when the kids were young and how tortuous it would be to go to a restaurant. It was as far from relaxing as you could get!

To be sitting in a restaurant 10 or 12 years later, laughing and telling stories or giving opinions about this, that and the other, makes my heart happy. It really is an example of seeing the profound in the ordinary — an ordinary day in an ordinary restaurant with an ordinary family — how rich!

TOOLS USED

1. Appreciate the daily rituals and daily richness of your lives.

2. Tell your children how enriched your life is simply because they are in it.

3. Point out all that you are grateful for in the life you are all sharing.

4. Make/create opportunities to spend time together with your teenager and engage him in conversations about large "life or world" issues.

5. Use ordinary moments to appreciate your teen and let him know how much you value time with him. It teaches him to appreciate the ordinary as well.

6. Do this regularly.

CHAPTER 15

Moving On

1. College Preparation

College preparation initially felt like a large black hole, filled with lots of things to do, forms to fill out, deadlines to meet, tests to be taken, a seemingly endless "to do" list with no notion of where our son would end up. What if he doesn't get outstanding test scores? What if he doesn't take the pre-ACT and SAT classes? What if he has no clue what he's interested in or where HE wants to go? What if what he wants is different from what we want for him? And, let's not forget the fact that Michael has a learning disability — do we only consider schools that have an official Learning Assistance Program?

All of these issues felt initially pretty overwhelming and some-what paralyzing. Wanting the best for our son, I didn't want to lose sight of the fact that a college choice is for and about him and not for and about me. So, that really meant making sure I paid attention to what Michael was thinking and wanting while at the same time keeping a balance between what he wanted and what we could afford.

Our first step in this process was to gather information — lots of it: information about the SAT, ACT, and financial aid. Obtaining information about those deadlines was very important and helped in making sure the prep work was being done. Also, the results from these tests and forms would narrow down options in terms of which college Michael could realistically attend.

Our second step was to go in to see the high school guidance counselor. She was very helpful in terms of telling us where Michael ranked in his class and where other students at his ranking had gone to college. She also had known Michael for two years and had a good sense of what kind of student and person he was, so she made suggestions regarding where he might go.

So, having that information helped narrow down the field. Next, we asked Michael where he was leaning. He was pretty clear in knowing: 1.) he wanted a Jesuit school since he was currently in one and liked their philosophy; 2.) he wanted a small or medium sized school of 8,000 students or less; 3.) he wanted some sort of learning assistance program; and 4.) he wanted to live not too far from home.

Well, that narrowed down the field considerably. Next came exploring small/medium Jesuit universities in the Midwest with learning assistance programs. The Princeton Book helped considerably with learning assistance programs selection and the Jesuit colleges.com website was also great.

Next came college visits. We tried to set up visits during the school year, but with basketball and end-of-the-year finals, that proved to be too big a task. So visits were made in summer. We visited four schools and at each one we paid attention to the following questions:

What was my original impression of the campus?
How did I feel when I was there?
What were the students like? Friendly or unfriendly?
Could I see myself on that campus?
Did they have activities in my area of interest?
How many students were commuting versus living on campus?
What was campus life like on the weekends?
Did they have a Learning Assistance Program that could meet my needs?
How accessible were the teachers?
How did the distance feel from home?

After asking these questions for all schools and visits, it became pretty clear that the school which kept rising to the top was Xavier University in Cincinnati, Ohio. So, after landing on this university, a second visit was planned which solidified his choice. That was followed by filling out an application for the school as well as three other "good enough" choices. Then we waited to see where all the applications and financial aid forms landed and what "packages" were offered, assuming acceptance by all four schools.

We just want to make sure that the fit between Michael and the school he wants works for our budget. And Michael needs to know that if his first choice doesn't work that he has to have a back-up choice or two that will also work for him. To me, the key in this process is all about preparation — doing your homework as both a parent and student to increase the probability of landing in the RIGHT school, not the BEST school — whatever that is — for your child, knowing that you are choosing among "good enough" schools.

TOOLS USED

1. Ask your child if he knows what he wants in terms of schools.

2. Gather SAT and ACT information during fall of junior year.

3. Keep a calendar, just for college deadlines, i.e. ACT, SAT tests, college application deadlines, etc.

4. Have your child take SAT, ACT prep courses. You don't have to hire someone — prep books are good enough.

5. Try to do college visits during his junior year so that senior year can be used for completing applications. Make sure your teen has visited the college he will attend.

6. Pace yourselves and remember that college "stuff" has to be done in addition to the regular demands of high school.

7. Keep checking with your senior to make sure deadlines are being met.

8. Remember, your teen is choosing among "good" things/ places and will land where he is supposed to.

9. Keep your sanity, above all else! There are lots of good schools that will take good care of your teen.

10. Sometimes the "best" universities are not the "best" places for your teen.

11. Keep a balanced perspective. Do not allow yourself to get "nuts" over this process.

2. The Beginnings of Leavings

It was May of Michael's senior year in high school and we were going to Xavier University for the weekend so that Michael could register for fall college classes. Here it is, I thought, the beginning of leavings. The beginning of Michael sitting down with an advisor and choosing his classes — him, not us and him. The beginning of him finding out where he will room and with whom — him, not us and him. The beginning of him deciding who to spend time with, how to spend his time, with not much direct accountability — again, him, not us and him.

For one of the first times, I really "get" how this is increasingly him and decreasingly, him and us. Oh, of course, I know we're still guiding and suggesting and expecting accountability, but it feels different now. Now he's going to be 325 miles away — 6 hours — "too far to just drop in," he says happily.

"Yes, too far to just drop in," I realize sadly.

He really is growing up and growing away — which is what he is supposed to do and what we are supposed to encourage him to do. And we do, but not without stretch marks — not without tweaks of sadness and times of excitement mixed together and yet sometimes very far apart.

And in-between are the tender times — the times when I see that although he is almost 18 years old, 6'3", 220 big pounds, he is still my son, my baby, who has his share of naivete and unworldliness that both endears him to me and makes me crazy.

Crazy is when we are en route to Xavier and Michael is driving. He is driving way too fast for my comfort, so I'm constantly yelling at him to slow down. He yells back that I'm distracting him from driving when I yell and could I please be quiet. I want to slap him upside the head when he does this and lecture him about safe driving techniques, especially since I am not with him most of the times he is driving the car. Instead I yell and tell him he's going to kill his Dad and me and then he'll feel guilty for the rest of his life. He rolls his eyes and assures me he knows exactly what he is doing and to stop trying to make him feel guilty — it's not working and is just annoying him. Crazy making!

The endearing part of him shows up when we get to the University. We had decided to stay on campus — in the dorm, to get the "full" experience. It was "full" all right — full of scarcity. The "suite" consisted of 2 dorm rooms, each with 2 beds and a living room/kitchen area in between. Cinder block walls, no decorations, 1 light blanket and sheet, pancake pillows and no hot water. No TV, no reading light, no rugs on the floor; just the basics, thank you very much. Michael was able to make fun of all of it in a very lighthearted way — was able to show he was a good sport, even though he would have preferred to spend the night in a nice hotel with a TV and a pool — endearing!

Or when he suggested we go out to eat off-campus instead of eating at the University. He knew of a really nice place — Penn Station — with really good food. Great, I think. He's taking charge, knows where to go. We'll eat at a nice restaurant and have some nice family time — a nice leisurely dinner, right? Wrong! We get to this place and it's basically a glorified Subway. Counter service and tiny booths. He thinks it's great. And, I must admit, the food was very good. It just wasn't what I was thinking when I imagined dinner "out." It was what an 18-year-old would picture. He was very proud of the fact that he knew his way around and HE was taking US — endearing! I could only smile and see that little boy of mine who wanted to please and who really did take good care of his parents — the beginnings of leavings as well as the beginning of beginnings — from the boy to the man!

TOOLS USED

1. Realize that when the time for "leaving" is on the horizon, you will probably start feeling ambivalent and/ or sad.

2. Give yourself permission to reminisce about the "good old days" with your teen as well as to anticipate life without your teen in your home.

3. Let yourself feel sad about what you are losing; i.e. face to face contact, daily influence and daily mothering tasks.

4. Let yourself get excited for your teen's next chapter of life and yours as well.

5. Begin to think about how you want to fill the space created by your teen's absence.

6. Take your time. Feel your feelings. Go through family photos and recall life with your son under your roof.

7. Talk to your friends about how you're feeling.

8. Remind yourself that because you did such a good job, your son is able and ready to fly off and be independent of you. That's a lot to feel proud about!

3. Bad Attitude or Style Difference?

I asked 18-year-old Andrew a question — a simple question. I don't even remember what the question was. But I do remember his response and it was full of "attitude." Readers may recognize this display — the eye-rolling, exasperated, what-do-you-want-from-me-now, tolerating me, kind of "attitude." And, lucky for me, he did this in front of two of his closest friends. I say lucky for me, because I decided to pull them into this scenario.

"OK," I said to Andrew, "let's stop the action right here."

"Steve and Pete, I'm going to ask your opinion now. I know you're Andrew's good friends and you are loyal to him, but help me out here. You just heard me ask Andrew a question and you heard his response. Did he or did he not answer me with a really bad attitude?"

They both started laughing. Andrew told them they didn't have to answer because he knew he didn't have any attitude with me. They responded by saying, "Sorry, Andrew, but, yeah, you had a bad attitude toward your Mom."

Andrew was shocked. He kept insisting that he answered my question with no attitude at all. Said his friends were nuts. I told him he should think about what his friends said, especially since he was so blind and in denial about how his tone of voice sounded. I told him I wished I had had a tape recorder so he could hear it himself.

We left the conversation at that point and he went off with his friends. I spent the rest of the day feeling sad and depressed and later lamented to Tom about it. Tom, in turn, unbeknownst to me, called Andrew and informed him that I was feeling bad about how we were relating to each other. He told Andrew to make a point of discussing and resolving the issue with me.

To his credit, Andrew did — the next morning. After he woke up, he came into the kitchen and said, "Mom, can we talk about what happened yesterday?"

I was startled, since Andrew typically does not initiate conversations like this. But, instead of pointing that out, I just said, "Sure, we can talk about it."

He said, "Why do you think this is happening with us?"

I replied, "Well, I think a lot of it is about the fact that you are leaving for college in a few weeks. I think you're anxious about that and maybe not even aware of how you're feeling about it. When people are in transition, which you and I are, they can have different reactions. Some people get sad, some people get mad, some people detach, some people withdraw, some people get overly attached and some people do all or some combination of the above."

"I think what's going on with us is that I am feeling sad about your leaving. Because I'm sad, I try harder and more often to make a connection with you. The way I do that is by asking questions. You experience my questions as intrusions or invasions. You get annoyed with me and respond with a bad attitude. I then get hurt or mad and act mad back at you. Then we part ways with both of us feeling annoyed and frustrated."

Andrew agreed and asked what we should do about it. I said I thought that this example also demonstrated that we had two different styles of communicating. My style is very direct —initiating conversations, asking questions, and seeking details. For example, when Andrew comes home after work, I'm right there, wanting details. "Hi honey," I say, "How are you? How was your day? What went on for you at work today?"

He interprets my attempts at "connection" as invasion and intrusion. His initial reaction is to withdraw and get away from me. As he describes it, "I've just worked all day. I want to come home, take a shower, relax a little by watching some TV. *Then* I want to have a conversation — not the very minute I come in the door."

When he responds like this, I feel rejected and hurt. Then I tend to ask more questions or probe more, instead of backing off.

So, we talked about these differences as "style" differences and he asked what I thought I could do about it. I suggested that we were already doing something about it by having this conversation. This would make us more aware of how to deal with it in the future. I also said that, because of these differences, it meant we would *BOTH* have to change our behavior. I would have to retreat some and not ask so many questions and he would have to initiate more so that I wouldn't end up chasing him for a connection.

"It doesn't take a lot," I said. "Just regular contact. If you initiate a conversation with me — tell me how you're doing, ask me about how I'm doing, go for a walk, a movie or otherwise engage with me — then I won't need to chase you."

Andrew really understood that. He nodded and said, "I can do that." And, to his credit, he has. After that conversation, he did initiate more conversations, invited me to dinner, a movie and asked me to take a few walks. All for short periods of time, but the point was that *he* was coming forward, *he* was initiating, *he* was doing some of the connecting. I, in turn, was much less intrusive. I stopped running after him to get information and got much less "attitude" from him as a result.

Our relationship is not perfect, but it sure is better. We understand each other more and we are much more aware of our personality differences. We both feel much more connected to one another. We have much less conflict and much more respect. We also have more fun. And because all of this happened just before the big college departure, I feel like it happened just in time! Just in time for both of us to feel better about the leaving.

TOOLS USED

1. Try to identify how you and your teen relate to one another. Are your communication styles similar or different? If they're similar, there may be no issue between you

both. If they are different, see if you can pinpoint those differences without making either one of you the "bad guy."

2. Talk with your teen about the similarities or differences in communication styles. Obviously, more conversation will be required when there are more differences than similarities. Normalize this — don't criticize or make it about your teen or something only he can change. Make this a team effort.

3. Discuss ways in which you can negotiate any differences. For example, if you are a "chaser" like me, then discuss ways in which you can "wait" or "hold back." If you hold back too much, discuss ways in which you can initiate or come forward.

4. Agree on some specific ways you can work to bridge the gap between you and your teen.

5. Check in with each other periodically and ask how you are doing from the other person's perspective.

6. Continue negotiating differences until you have found a "middle" ground that works for both of you.

4. One More Layer of Letting Go

I expected to cry and I didn't. I searched in all the corners and all I could find was gratitude. It surprised me. And comforted me.

We had taken our 18-year-old for the 6-hour drive to Cincinnati, Ohio, his soon-to-be new college home. Finally, this was the weekend we would let him go — out of our home and into the arms of strangers. Could I do it without heartache and sadness? I really didn't know. I had begun to tick off the days — the last Monday we would be together as a family, the last Tuesday we would have a family meal, the last Wednesday, etc. So I had been practicing "sad" for a number of days/weeks.

And, finally, here it was — the actual leaving. Packing the van up with all of the things he would "need." Knowing that we would be coming home with an empty van — but mostly, without Michael. And so, I imagined sad. Imagined I would need a lot of support from my husband and from my friends. Imagined I'd walk past Michael's room and feel sad and empty. Imagined I would throw all of my excess time and energy into 15-year-old Andrew — poor kid!

But, it didn't turn out that way — not at all. I was first struck by how wonderful this school was going to be when we arrived on moving day. As we reached the front of the line at Michaels' new dorm, there were about 40 students, all wearing sky blue t-shirts, clapping and cheering as each car stopped to be unloaded. The new student was asked his name, a cheer and clapping from the crowd happened, followed by 40 kids emptying out our van and taking Michael's "stuff" to his new room. Unloaded in less than 5 minutes and we, not having to lift a finger, much less carry a load! What kind of a welcome was that? I'll tell you what kind — wonderful!

As if that wasn't enough, the atmosphere all around the campus was one of friendliness and helpfulness — aiming to please — aiming to help you feel welcome — and we did. From the university President's welcoming speech to the "talks" we attended, the welcoming mass followed by the welcoming reception, the tone was one of embracing, of letting us know that our son would not only be in safe hands, but in loving hands. And I believed it — believed it because I felt it –believed it because I saw my son experience it. I saw him jump in with both feet and I saw him on his own — and doing well.

What more could I, as a parent, want for him? To know that he would be in a thriving, stimulating environment with care all around him, surrounded by people who would have his best interest at heart — what could be better than that? Nothing, I thought. Nothing. So what should I feel sad about? Nothing, I decided. Nothing, except perhaps that I wanted to go there myself — wanted to be able to experience all of that again — only from the vantage point of who I am now — not who I was then. I would have a greater appreciation for it now.

But I will have to settle for having an appreciation that my son will be the one to experience it now and that my job is to let him go, and be grateful that he will be cared for well. What more could a mother want? Nothing... so I have no tears, no sadness — only gratitude!

TOOLS USED

1. Don't be surprised if you don't feel sad as you drop your teen off at college. You may get all of your sadness done before he leaves. Either way, give yourself permission to feel whatever comes up for you.

2. Let your teen know how excited you are for him as he enters this new chapter of life. And also let him know that you will miss him.

3. Leave a card or note in his room as you depart, letting him know how proud you are of him and how you know he will do well.

5. Back And Forth

He's 20 now. He's a junior in college. He comes home to visit. He goes back to college. He comes home to visit or to work for the summer. He goes back to college. That's been the ritual for the past 3 years — back and forth; back and forth. He's here. Then he's not.

So what can we expect in this "in-between" time — this back and forth time? How do you parent when your teen is on their own most of the time and under your roof for only some of the time? What are the rules for the "in-between?"

This is usually the scenario; Michael leaves in August for college; he comes home at Thanksgiving, Christmas, and maybe spring break and then is home for the summer. When he's home, he visits with us the first evening — until about 10 p.m., when we get tired and go off to sleep. He then calls his friends, they come over and they all go out to the popular bars. They take a cab, so no drinking and driving. Good! They come home about 2, 3, or 4 a.m. and crash in the basement. He's usually quiet, so we aren't awakened. Sometimes he will bring a bunch of friends with him, male and female. Girls in the bedroom, boys in the family room. All nice kids. No trouble. No drama. Just back and forth; in and out. Having group fun. Emphasis on getting together as a group, going out to a bar or a game or a party or something social — often drinking, then coming home, and not necessarily to their own home. Just somebody in "the group's" home — crashing — sleeping late, then going home — to their own homes. And starting it all over again.

This pattern is a repetition of their life at college — with studying of various degrees being done in-between social activities. When at home, the in-between social activities means time with us, the parents, but we are definitely not the focal point of the "time-off." We are "home base," the place they love to come to for food, rest, TV time, conversation and checking-in — all of that being done in-between the all important friend/socializing network. It reminds me of when they were 2-years-old and would go off exploring their little worlds for a while, but would always have to come back to us to touch home base before running off again.

As I watch this, I wonder if we are doing our kids a disservice by allowing all of this "fun"? Shouldn't they be working harder or more or staying in more and acting like responsible adults? Maybe. But when I listen to them and watch them and see how and who they are in the world, I think, "Good for them!" This is a fabulous time in their lives. They have the security of home, the privilege of going away to school, working a little and really enjoying the friendship connections that being at college allows. This is a time in their lives that will feed them later. A time they'll reach back to when responsibilities weigh in, when friends have dispersed to different places in the world, when having fun is secondary to working hard to provide instead of being provided for.

As Michael said to me during his most recent visit, "Mom, I'm really appreciating this time in college. Come next year I know my life will be different. I won't be able to just go out with friends and have fun or go off to Rome for a semester or have 4 weeks off at Christmas and all that other good stuff. I'll soon be living like you and Dad do, and, don't get me wrong, that looks good to me too, but there's nothing like "now" — this is the best!"

He's right — it is the best — and what I know about that is the fact that Michael gets it. He appreciates it, and he knows that when he's done with college, he will move into a whole different dimension of life. And he'll be ready for that when it comes. And he'll do that part well, too. But for now, he's appreciating another privilege being given to him by us and is valuing it. He knows that this is a very special time in his life and is making the most of it. And I am truly happy to provide it because ultimately, I know it is a wonderful preparation for the world he will enter when he's done with college — the one we commonly refer to as "the REAL world." And he'll be ready for it. For now, though, he's enjoying his "utopia" and I am enjoying the back and forth!

TOOLS USED

1. Make sure when your teen comes home during these "in-between" times that you have predictable family time.

2. Check in, getting the details that you miss in their lives and they miss in yours. Linger in the "catching up."

3. Let them know the expectations regarding being in your home, even if they are only "visiting"; i.e. no curfew, but check-in when you arrive or call and leave a message if you're not coming home.

4. Be clear about any expectations regarding opposite sex visitors; i.e. sleeping in separate rooms.

5. Remind them of any chores they are still expected to do, even though they are only here for a "visit."

6. Remind them of how special this in-between time is for them — and for you, since it allows you as a parent to gradually let go of them and they of you.

6. The Hesitation

At the end of our phone call, I asked 20-year-old Michael if he missed me. I knew I shouldn't, but I asked anyway. He hesitated before saying, "Uh, of course I do, Ma."

"No, you don't," I laughed, "and you're not supposed to." We both laughed then, only my laugh was more melancholy than his.

Michael's hesitation told me a lot. Here he is, one week into a five-week journey to Rome and having the time of his life. He is taking three classes, seeing the sights, learning about old and new cultures, making new friends and broadening his horizons. The time of *his* life.

This time, however, in *my* life, feels different. I keep being reminded of leavings. My "almost" 21-year-old leaving for Italy, my 18-year-old leaving high school. Both of them leaving me. Leaving in the best way — to go on *in* their lives, *with* their lives, on *into* different facets of their lives — without me at the helm. With *them* at the helm and their Dad and I watching from the shoreline, no longer on the boat *with* them, no longer directing the boat, but cheering them from a distance, watching them from a distance.

I'm not sure how to do this separation thing. I feel myself floundering; sometimes focused on new things that are just for me; sometimes excited about new adventures with my husband without the kids; sometimes just sad about what my place in the world is now. Now that one son is a senior in college. Now that the other son is a freshman in college. Now that they have rightfully put us in another place. It's like being put in another location on the mantle. Instead of front and center, we've been moved to the side — still important but no longer central. Only central when something goes wrong or is needed. Otherwise, we get short "check-in" calls, short visits, updates about classes, friends, work, etc. But mostly my boys are busy now — too busy to call and too busy to linger. It reminds me of when the boys were two. They would use us as a "touchstone" — wanted to know that we were around but only long enough to see us. Then they would turn right around and get "busy" again.

So, here they are, busy in their lives — happy in their lives. And I am proud and happy *for* and *with* them. Their happiness and wellness in the world is, in part, a tribute to their Dad and me. Our involvement paid off — they are good people in the world — capable people in the world and increasingly independent people in the world. And we helped get them there. We did our job so well that they need us less and less.

Yippee! We were successful. So successful, we're pretty much out of a job now! So why do I feel so ambivalent? Why do I feel at a loss? Why? I guess because they were *my* "touchstone." They were my "busy-ness" for so long that I'm not sure how or where to point my energy right now, or how to get "busy" doing something else that has meaning for me, being someone other than "Mom." Of course, I know I'll always be "Mom" to my kids and they will always have a place in my life, but I am very aware that once they leave for school, our relationship with each other changes. Changes because it has to. Changes because they have to take on greater and greater degrees of caring for themselves in ways that their Dad and I have cared for them up to this time. And I want them to do that. I'm just not sure what I am going to do in the meantime.

So, what I do in this "in-between" time is to look forward to spending those time fragments with my kids whenever I can get them. I enjoy spending those five minutes with 18-year-old Andrew, "in-between" his engagements, in-between his busy-ness, in-between work and friends. Or when Michael comes home on school breaks and we go out to dinner or catch a movie or talk for a few minutes before he meets up with his friends. I am so aware that the primary focus for them is spending time with their friends, not spending time with me and their Dad. And, while I know and can celebrate that, I also know that I would gladly spend a lot more time with them if they asked. But they won't because it's not really what they want to do, nor is it what they should do. Oh, I know sometimes they will spend more time with me because they know I'm still trying to find my place — my new place — on the mantel. I'm working on it and I know I'll arrive at some new and interesting destinations. But, for now, I'm feeling the impact of having been moved to a different place on the parenting board. I'm just not sure how to play this part of the game. But I'll learn. I always do — and this time my kids are the ones who are teaching *me* how to do it!

TOOLS USED

1. Acknowledge if/when you have gotten upset with your teen about "leavings." Make sure you let him know that it is probably *you*, not him, who is having a problem. If both of you share this problem, then acknowledge that.

2. Be able to let you teen know that you are sad about his leaving but that he is not responsible for taking care of you. *You* will take care of you. His job is to keep moving on in his life.

3. Have compassion for yourself if you are feeling lost or struggling with what's next for you. Give yourself time to "try on" different options.

4. Keep in touch with your teen during your transition but give him the space that he needs/desires/requests.

5. Don't "guilt trip" your teen into feeling responsible for not taking "care" of you when what he needs to focus on is leaving you.

6. Do ask your teen how *he* feels about leaving you, his home, his friends and all that is familiar. Learn to share your feelings with each other but be sure to avoid eliciting guilt in your teen.

SUMMARY

Top Ten Tools For Better Parenting

1. Listen, Listen, Listen

This is probably the most important tool in the box of parenting skills discussed in this book.

Listening does not mean "agreeing" with your teen. PLEASE GET THIS, PARENTS! It means *hearing* what he is saying and letting him know that you have heard him. It is not (necessarily) agreeing with what he is saying.

Agreeing is separate and distinct from hearing.

Do Not Put Them Together!

The more your teen feels "heard," the less he has to rebel against.

A specific method of *"Hearing"* is to:

Repeat Back to Your Teen What He Has
Just Said to You — Without Commentary.

You must "hear" him without telling him what you think or feel about what he just said.

If your teen says, "I don't care what you say, I'm staying out as long as my friends do," then you may say in response, "So, regardless of what I say, you plan on staying out as late as your friends do — did I understand that right?"

After that comment, you can get into specifics about your different points of view, but at least you start off with some level of understanding and your teen doesn't have to keep trying to get you to hear him.

I cannot stress enough the importance of this particular tool. It goes a long way in the art of communicating with your teenager and can minimize a WHOLE lot of arguing — try it and you'll see!

2. Talk, Talk, Talk

Talk to your teen. Talk about small things — talk about big things, but make sure you talk to him and talk to him everyday.

If you're unsure what to talk about, try asking him. If he doesn't "help" you out, then talk about the news or talk about the latest book you read or the TV show you watched or the kind of day you just had.

Talk to him about what you like about him, i.e. "Have I told you lately how much I appreciate having you as my son?" or "I really like that you helped out with the dishes tonight." Or "Thanks for doing your homework without my having to yell at you."

Create opportunities to compliment your teen: "That shirt looks great on you," or "That cologne smells good," or just, "You look great!"

Shift your focus from the negative to the positive: "I really like it when we get along, don't you?"

Look your teen in the eye when you talk and ask the same of him. It's amazing what you notice when you are actually looking at each other and how much better communication goes when that is happening.

Even if/when you get single-word responses, keep asking.

Ask him specific questions:

How was your day today?

Tell me one thing you learned at school today.

Who are you hanging out with?

What are you doing when you're out?

If you go to someone's home, is there an adult present?

Is your homework done?

Are your chores done?

Did you have some fun today?

Did you hear that story on the news about …?

Tell me the five best and five worst things that happened to you today.

Besides being interested in his life, teach him to ask about yours as well. Teenagers can be very self-centered, so they need to learn how to show interest in others.

Offer information about yourself. Tell him about your day, your life, your growing up, your opinion. Give him a sense about who you are even if he doesn't appear interested. He is. And don't do it as a lecture, but as a conversation.

Remember, this is not only an opportunity to teach him about how to relate to you, it's also a time to connect with him in a way that's not about telling him what he is doing wrong.

3. Teach, Teach, Teach … Model, Model, Model

Let your teen know what your values are. If you believe your teen should not drink until he is 21 "simply" because it's against the law, let him know that. Don't apologize for it even if your teen thinks you're a "dork."

If you believe in no sex before marriage, say so. Don't hedge. And let him know how you arrived at that decision. It helps him realize that decisions are often made over time and as the result of experiences, both positive and negative.

Don't leave "big ticket" items up to him to decide on his own. It really helps him to have a blueprint, even though he may have you believe he doesn't need one.

If you believe in "safe sex" let him know that and provide him with both information and contraception.

In other words, as an adult/parent who knows how to think about the consequences of one's behavior, you can set parameters/ boundaries with your teen in order to provide him with some guidelines, even if he decides not to follow them. For instance, you can have rules like "no overnights with girlfriends" or "no one of the opposite sex is allowed in your room with the door closed."

Because teens often have a hard time saying "no" on their own for fear of looking like "wimps" or disappointing their friends, occasionally they need adults to be the "bad guys." Sometimes they need to be able to blame us when (or if) they're not strong enough on their own. Until they are capable and ready to make more mature decisions, it is our job as parents to set the rules and guidelines for them. Remember, we can't make them follow these rules. But we can make sure that they understand the rules as well as the consequences for failure to follow them. Understanding rules and consequences is not only good for them, it is good for us as well. Part of our parenting job is to guide and model for them the job of being an adult. Remember, if they're not getting the modeling from you, they will be getting it from the "outside" somewhere, and you have no control over what they will take when they are looking. Help them out by offering a frame of reference they can trust — give them a blueprint of your beliefs and values. Even if they make choices different from yours — they might, and that's O.K. — they still will have something concrete to hold onto.

4. Help, Help, Help

As a parent, if you are unsure of what to do or how to handle a situation, look for resources to help you. Don't expect to know all the answers. Seek out help. That help can take the form of:

Other parents. Ask others how they handled similar situations and/or what they would do in your situation.

Books. Go to the bookstore or library and look for resources and/or ask friends if they can recommend books they have found helpful.

Professionals. If you need help figuring out how to parent better or you need information or intervention regarding substance abuse for your teen, search for a professional to help you. Consider your family medical doctor, a minister, a priest, a school counselor, a social worker, a psychologist, or a psychiatrist. Remember, if you had a broken arm, you wouldn't hesitate to go to a doctor. Likewise, if you have a fractured family, go to someone who can help you mend it. It's nothing to be ashamed of.

5. Show Up, Show Up, Show Up

Continue to stay involved with your teen's interests, whether or not you like what he is interested in.

If he is involved in a sport, show up at his games, even if he tells you it doesn't matter. It does.

If he is involved in the arts or in theatre, attend performances and/or ask him what he is doing. Have him show you if he has something he has made or designed.

If he doesn't have any outside activities, involve him in your life. Invite him out with you to dinner, to a ball game, to a movie. Play a board game, play cards, go shopping, or go out for a walk. Do anything that demonstrates you care about him and wish to have him be an important part of your life

If he doesn't have organized activities, express interest in whatever else he does — it might be shopping or computer games or something you know nothing about. But regardless, be sure to ask!

Encourage, explore, nudge — try anything and everything to find a point of connection, no matter how small or insignificant it may appear. You may need to help your teen develop in new areas since teenage interests often aren't the same as those of younger children. Work with him to help him find hobbies and activities if these don't come easily. Hang in there with him!

6. Know, Know, Know

Know your teen's friends. Make sure you meet whomever your teen is spending time with and make sure you know what he is doing as well as where he is doing it.

Create an environment that encourages your teen to be at your home. If possible, make your house the "go to" house. Have lots of snacks and a place for them to hang out. In our case, we saved the basement for socializing and put up a basketball hoop in the alley for the kids to hang out at. And we always have LOTS of snacks!

If your house is the "hub," make it a point to spend a few minutes talking with your teen's friends. Show an interest in them and what they are doing. Don't be an "interrogator," just ask basic questions like, "How are you doing?, How's school going?" or "Doing anything extra after school?" or "How about those Cubs?"

If your house isn't the "hub," ask your teen to bring kids by so you can meet them. Don't let them get away with always going out and meeting with friends you have never met. Be insistent.

If your teen hangs at someone else's house, make sure you get to know the parents to make sure adequate supervision is provided.

7. Awareness, Awareness, Awareness

Understand that the way you were raised necessarily affects your parenting style. Be willing to look at how this gets in your way as well as how it helps you.

Be able to identify the "garbage" and the "gold" you came in with from the family you were raised in.

Examples of "Garbage" include:

Having an alcoholic parent and assuming that if your teenager drinks at all, he will become an alcoholic. So you, as a parent, overreact any time this issue comes up. In this scenario, it's important to understand that just because your parent was an alcoholic, it doesn't necessarily mean your teenager is one if he picks up a drink. It's certainly possible, but overreacting is the result of what you experienced growing up, not necessarily what your teen is doing now. Furthermore, overreacting can create what you fear most, rather than resolving the problem. A better solution is to sit and talk about it with your teen at a time when emotions are not running high and no one has been drinking. And tell your teen that the reason you feel so strongly about this issue is because you were raised with an alcoholic parent and you fear this for him.

If drinking/drug use is an issue, make sure you look at your own usage and the modeling you're doing for your teenager. Obviously, if you drink a lot and you tell your teen not to, there's a credibility gap and that becomes a problem. Do you really expect your teen to do what *you* won't? Practice what you preach or what you preach simply won't be heard! Clean up your own act; then talk to your teen about cleaning up his!

If you were raised by a parent who was either too liberal or too rigid, then your own parenting style may either imitate your upbringing or tend to the opposite extreme because you felt your own parents were either too permissive or too restrictive. A better solution is to acknowledge the flawed environment in which you were raised. Find a middle ground that balances the two extremes rather than simply repeating or rejecting them.

If you have leftover resentments toward your parents from growing up, identify those feelings and get rid of them by writing, talking or seeking professional help. Don't carry that forward to contaminate your current family.

Examples of "Gold" include:

Identifying those values you learned while growing up and that you would like to continue to carry on in your "today" family.

Imitating the rituals that you loved while growing up and adding them to your "today" family.

Taking the best qualities from both of your parents and adding those qualities and skills to your own parenting toolbox.

8. Love 'Em, Love 'Em, Love 'Em

Hug your teen regularly. If he gets too embarrassed or too resistant, hug him in your home when no one is around, but hug him. Touch is a very important ingredient and an important tool for parents to use. It can soothe a lot of hurt and bridge a lot of pain.

If your teen won't hug you or you yourself are not physical, either practice getting better at it or touch them on the shoulder or pat them on the back on a regular basis. The emphasis needs to be "on a regular basis."

Say, "I love you" frequently. If it doesn't come easily, then practice until it does! Say, "I love you" out loud — a number of times. It may feel awkward at first, but the more you practice, the easier it will get and the better it will feel, to you and to them!

Your children are your treasures — that never changes. Let them know that is forever true, even when you get very upset with them or feel distant from them or they from you. In our household we always say, "Goodnight, I love you, goodnight" and hug and kiss each other before going to bed, no matter how we may feel toward each other at the moment. No one goes to bed without those words being spoken. That reminds us that we are connected to each other and love each other, even if we get mad at each other. And it teaches teens about how to act like mature, healthy adults. In other words, our love for each other is not dependent on our moods or on our teens' good behavior. We don't have to "like" each other to "love" each other.

9. Mistakes, Mistakes, Mistakes

Know you will make them. Lots of them. With great and consistent regularity. Count on it.

Learn from your mistakes. Twelve-step programs teach that the definition of insanity is doing the same thing over and over again, each time expecting a different end result. In other words, if you try some or any parenting tool with your teens over and over again and it doesn't work, give it up. Stop it! Get or try a different tool. Don't expect to get a different result from your teen. Remember, you're the adult. You must be the one to try a different approach or a different tool, not your teenager. If you do, it absolutely, positively increases your chances of getting a different result from your teenager. While there are no guarantees, you have nothing to lose by trying something different and everything to gain if you do!

When you make a mistake with your teen, apologize! He needs to hear "I'm sorry" when you have done something wrong or hurtful. Not only is it the right thing to do, it's also good role modeling to let him know that we all make mistakes. The "job" is all about how you handle mistakes when you make them as well as learning not to repeat them!

10. Laugh, Laugh, Laugh

Teenagers love to laugh! Just watch any group of them and what are they most likely to be doing? Laughing; kidding with each other; joking with each other; making fun of each other. As much as you can as a parent, laugh with them. Find a way to bring humor into your encounters with them. Not only does it smooth the waters of communication, but they actually learn a lot through humor. I recall being on vacation in Arkansas recently with my 16-year-old son. He and a friend had gone to a "teen night" gathering at one of the pools at the resort we were staying at. Apparently, he was swearing a lot during the activity and a little 80-year-old lady, who overheard him, came up to him, grabbed him by the cheeks, smiled and said, "Young man, you have a dirty mouth. If I hear you cuss one more time, I'm gonna take my sock off and stuff it right here in your mouth! Understand?" Andrew nodded and chuckled about it, and promptly stopped swearing. And he couldn't wait to report the story back to us. Thought it was hysterical — but he got it. And do you know that every time he saw that woman again during our trip, they would smile, wave at each other and she would say, "Remember, young man, I still got that sock ready for ya if you don't keep your mouth clean!" And Andrew would smile, shake his head and promise that he would keep his mouth clean! He was able to hear her because she used humor. If it had been done seriously, he probably would have either disregarded the advice or been defiant about it and sworn even more! And please don't hear that I'm advocating that humor be used all the time — I'm not. However, I do think that we, as parents, don't use it nearly enough and should remember that humor can be a very effective tool along with all the others in that parenting box!

CONCLUSION

If you practice the above principles on a regular basis, you will do a better job of parenting. The key word here is PRACTICE. Remember, parenting is a combination of adding the "good stuff" from the family you were raised in, subtracting the "bad stuff" from that family, and going out and learning some "new stuff," all of which will give you the "best stuff," the skills you will need to do the complex job of raising your teenagers with the best parenting toolbox you can put together! — all the while, of course, knowing that the road is rife with potholes, mistakes, detours, etc. However, working on your end of it is the best preparation you can make for yourselves and for your teen in order to be able to do the hardest, most frustrating, most heartbreaking, most exhilarating and most rewarding job in the world — parenting!

Index

191

T

ABOUT THE AUTHOR

Gale Dreas has been a Clinical Social Worker for 24 years and a parent for 21 years. Earlier in her career, she worked for Lutheran Social Services of Illinois and specialized in the area of substance abuse/addiction. She was the Director of Outpatient Services for the Women's Residence of Lutheran Social Services and subsequently went into Private Practice, where she has been working for the past 20 years. Prior to becoming a Social Worker, she was also a police officer, where she learned how to appreciate, value and strive for the "normal" aspects of life.

For more information, please see
www.galedreas.com

The Dreas/Brennan Family
Andrew, Gale, Tom and Michael in Rome, Italy, Summer 2006

Printed in the United States
74948LV00005B/109-111